THE WORLD OF
Saint Patrick

THE WORLD OF
Saint Patrick

Philip Freeman

OXFORD
UNIVERSITY PRESS

OXFORD

UNIVERSITY PRESS

Oxford University Press is a department of the
University of Oxford. It furthers the University's objective
of excellence in research, scholarship, and education
by publishing worldwide.

Oxford   New York

Auckland   Cape Town   Dar es Salaam   Hong Kong   Karachi
Kuala Lumpur   Madrid   Melbourne   Mexico City   Nairobi
New Delhi   Shanghai   Taipei   Toronto

With offices in

Argentina   Austria   Brazil   Chile   Czech Republic   France   Greece
Guatemala   Hungary   Italy   Japan   Poland   Portugal   Singapore
South Korea   Switzerland   Thailand   Turkey   Ukraine   Vietnam

Oxford is a registered trade mark of Oxford University Press
in the UK and certain other countries.

Published in the United States of America by
Oxford University Press
198 Madison Avenue, New York, NY 10016

Library of Congress Cataloging-in-Publication Data
Freeman, Philip, 1961–
The world of Saint Patrick / Philip Freeman.
pages cm
Includes bibliographical references and index.
ISBN 978-0-19-937258-4 (hardcover : alk. paper)—
ISBN 978-0-19-937259-1 (ebook)—ISBN 978-0-19-937260-7 (ebook)
1. Patrick, Saint, 373?-463?   2. Christian saints—Ireland—Biography.
3. Ireland—Church history—To 1172.   4. Brigid, of Ireland, Saint,
approximately 453-approximately 524.   5. Brendan, Saint,
the Voyager, approximately 483–577.   I. Title.
BR1720.P26F76   2014
270.2092—dc23
[B]
2013049359

1 3 5 7 9 8 6 4 2

Printed in the United States of America
on acid-free paper

CONTENTS

PREFACE

The World of Saint Patrick is a collection of the oldest and best sources on the beginnings of Christianity in Ireland. The two letters written by Patrick himself are the earliest documents in this collection, but also of great value are the decrees, hymns, prayers, and stories that grew up around him in the centuries immediately after his death. Of the greatest importance as well for understanding this time are the life story of Brigid, the earliest woman saint of Ireland, and the tale of the voyage of Brendan across the unknown sea in search of a land promised to the saints.

The modest purpose of this small book is to gather together for the first time the most important sources on early Irish Christianity for readers interested in this remarkable period of history. All the translations have been made from the original Latin and Old Irish sources with attention to both accuracy and accessibility. The introductions have been kept to a necessary minimum so that the documents may speak for themselves.

Many thanks to the American Academy of Religion, the National Endowment for the Humanities, and the libraries of Harvard Divinity School, the Institute for Advanced Study at Princeton, the National Library of Ireland, and Luther College for their help in the creation of this book. My gratitude as well to Lisa Bitel and Dorothy Bray for reading through the manuscript and to the many kind friends throughout Ireland who guided me in my research and showed me such hospitality. But my greatest thanks are to my students in my courses on early Irish Christianity over the years, who have made my own exploration of this long-ago world so enjoyable.

THE
WESTERN
SEA

ULSTER

Sliab
Miss ∧

Armagh

Saul

CONNACHT

Boyne R.

Tara

Shannon
R.

Kildare

Liffey R.

THE
EASTERN
SEA

Aran
Islands

LEINSTER

MUNSTER

IRELAND

THE WORLD OF
Saint Patrick

SAINT PATRICK'S LETTER TO THE SOLDIERS OF COROTICUS

No one knows when the people of the Mediterranean world first heard of Ireland. The first report probably dates back to the late sixth century BC, though it survives only in a garbled form recorded eight hundred years later in a Roman poem called the *Ora Maritima*. The poem states that a place called the Sacred Isle, rich in turf, lies far away in the distant sea and is inhabited by a people called the *Hierni*. The Greek explorer Pytheas from the colony of Massalia (modern Marseille, France) probably visited Ireland in the late fourth century BC, but his account of the voyage didn't survive intact. By the early first century of our era, the classical world certainly knew of Ireland—which they called *Ierne* or *Hibernia*—but they knew only that it was an island smaller than Britain and reportedly inhabited by uncivilized cannibals. By the time of the historian Tacitus and the geographer Ptolemy in the late first and second centuries AD, merchants had brought back considerable information about the island, so much so that the Roman general Agricola considered invading it from his base in Britain. About AD 200, the Roman author Solinus records that Ireland was inhabited by a warlike people, but that the island had no snakes. From that date to the end of the Roman Empire, the few references to Ireland in classical sources are largely complaints that the island was a land of savages who brought terror to the good people of Roman Britain with their vicious attacks and pirate raids.

In spite of the biased reports about Ireland from classical sources, we can be sure that Ireland was no more barbaric than any other land on the borders of the Roman world. Later Irish sources reveal that it was divided into more than a hundred independent tribes each ruled by a *rí* or king. The lords and warriors of the island ruled over small-scale farmers who based their worth on the number of cattle they owned. Fighting between tribes was frequent, but most of the Irish lived quiet lives growing their crops and raising their animals. Women had more legal rights than in ancient Greece or Rome, but they were still subordinate to men, though a wife could divorce her husband if he was abusive or became too fat for sexual intercourse.

The inhabitants of ancient Ireland worshipped many gods and goddesses, each with particular areas of expertise, much like those of the Greeks and Romans. The god Lug, known across Celtic Europe, was a divinity of many skills who was honored at his festival of Lugnasad in early August. Other gods included the paternal Dagda, his son Oengus, and Ogma the patron of poets. Among the many goddesses were numbered Danu, the divine mother, the beautiful Fann and Lí Ban, and Brigid, a goddess of wisdom and prophecy who shares many qualities with the later saint of the same name. The priests of the Irish were the druids, who had also been present in Britain and continental Europe. The druids included in their many skills the performance of sacrifice and prophecy.

At the opposite end of the known world at the beginning of the first century, a new religion sprang forth from the ancient traditions of Judaism and began to spread across the Roman Empire. Christianity was quickly established in the cities of the empire, but it was only a small and sometimes persecuted cult until the emperor Constantine adopted the faith as his own in the early fourth century. At about the same time, the small groups of celibate Christian men and women who had gathered in informal communities to pursue their spiritual goals gave way to larger, more organized groups. The pioneers in this movement were Anthony and Pachomius in Egypt, who organized the first monasteries in the desert based on work and worship governed by a common rule. This sort of group ascetic life soon spread throughout the Near East, then west to Italy, Spain, and Gaul. From the beginning, communities of women were an important part of the monastic movement.

Christianity was probably established in Britain by the third century and there may have been missions to Ireland as early as the fourth century, but the earliest account of the new faith on the island is a statement from the chronicler Prosper who says that in the year 431 Pope Celestine ordained the deacon Palladius and sent him to Ireland as a bishop to serve the Christians who were already there. The flock Palladius ministered to may have consisted primarily of Christians captured in Britain and transported against their will to Ireland as slaves.

The story of Patricius, better known as Saint Patrick, is preserved in two short Latin letters which he himself wrote in his old age. In these invaluable documents, Patrick describes himself as a Briton of the Roman nobility who was kidnapped from his family villa by pirates and taken to Ireland when he was about sixteen. His grandfather had been a priest and his father a deacon, so Patrick had been raised as a Christian, but he had rejected his childhood faith and become an atheist by his early teens. Nonetheless, several years of brutal slavery in Ireland turned him into a fervent believer who heard the voice of God telling him to flee back to Britain. Against all odds and with the help of reluctant Irish merchants, Patrick escaped to Britain, only to hear the voice of God again and return to Ireland as a missionary to the very people who had enslaved him. His letters tell of many difficulties both with the Irish and with church authorities in Britain, but he had some measure of success during his many years in Ireland converting natives to the new religion.

The first of the two works of Patrick is the *Letter to the Soldiers of Coroticus*, a scathing denunciation of a British warlord named Coroticus and his men who had recently raided Ireland and either killed or kidnapped into slavery a number of Patrick's recent Irish converts. It is a forceful letter of excommunication backed by frequent quotations from scripture threatening Coroticus and his men with eternal damnation if they did not return their captives. Whether or not the letter was effective we do not know.

The second surviving document from the hand of Patrick is traditionally called the *Confession*, although it is more of a declaration than an act of contrition. The audience of the letter is primarily the British bishops who have called Patrick home from Ireland to face charges of corruption and to answer for an unknown sin he committed when he was a teenager. Patrick carefully explains to the bishops and his other readers why he is innocent of any wrongdoing and why he refuses to return to Britain. Woven into the letter are many biographical details of his early life and experiences as a missionary in Ireland.

The *Letter to the Soldiers of Coroticus* and *Confession* provide modern readers with a rare glimpse into a time and place for which there are few other sources. They also are a particularly revealing look into the heart and mind of a man who lived long ago.

The dates of Patrick are uncertain, but most scholars would agree that the traditional arrival of Patrick in Ireland in 432 and his death in either 461 or 463 are not far from the mark. The language and historical references in the letters fit well with dates of composition somewhere in the latter half of the fifth century.

The standard edition of Patrick's Latin letters is Ludwig Bieler *Libri Epistolarum Sancti Patricii Episcopi*. Richard P. C. Hanson and Cécile Blanc's Latin/French edition, *Confession et la Lettre à Coroticus*, is also quite good. Older, but still valuable, is Newport White's *Libri Sancti Patricii*.

There are a number of excellent translations of Patrick's letters available, most of which contain helpful introductions and notes. Ludwig Bieler's *The Works of St. Patrick* and Thomas O'Loughlin's *Discovering Saint Patrick* are particularly helpful.

Two excellent studies of Patrick's life are Richard P. C. Hanson, *Saint Patrick: His Origins and Career,* and E. A. Thompson, *Who Was Saint Patrick?* There is also my own *St. Patrick of Ireland.* A helpful collection of essays related to Patrick and his letters is found in David Dumville, *Saint Patrick: A.D. 493–1993.*

I am Patrick, a sinner and very ignorant man. I declare that I have been appointed as a bishop in Ireland—and I believe that I have received this position from God himself. I live as a stranger and exile here among barbarians and pagans because of my love for God. He is my witness that this is true.

I have never wanted to speak harshly and sternly, but the zeal of God and the truth of Christ have forced me to do it for the sake of my neighbors and children, for whom I gave up my homeland, my family, and my very life until my death.[1] I live for my God to teach unbelievers, if I am worthy, even if some people hate me.

I have composed and written these words with my own hand, to be taken, sent, and delivered to the soldiers of Coroticus.[2] I don't call them my countrymen or blessed Roman citizens, because by their evil deeds they have become fellow citizens with demons.[3] They act in the same way as our enemies and live in death as allies of the Irish and the apostate Picts.[4] They are blood-thirsty men yearning for the blood of innocent Christians, the very ones I brought to life in God and confirmed in Christ.

The day after these men cruelly cut down with their swords my newly baptized—they were still clothed in their white garments and had anointing oil on their foreheads—I sent a letter to them by the hand of a holy priest I had trained since his youth, along with some clerics.[5] I asked that they return the baptized captives along with some of the goods they had stolen, but they laughed at them.

I don't know who I should weep for more, whether it be the ones killed, those captured, or the men trapped so completely in the devil's snares. Together with Satan they will suffer eternal punishment in hell. For whoever commits sin is the slave of sin and will be known as a child of the devil.[6]

So let all who fear God know that these men are strangers to me and to Christ my God, the one I serve as an ambassador.[7] They are murderers of fathers and brothers, ravaging wolves who devour the people of God as if they were bread.[8] As scripture says: "The wicked have destroyed your law, O Lord,"[9] the same law that our merciful and kind God has established in Ireland in these last days.

I am not exceeding my authority for I am one of those men God has called and predestined to preach the gospel in the face of terrible persecutions to the very ends of the earth,[10] even if our enemy shows his jealousy through the tyrant Coroticus, a man with no respect for God or his priests. For God has chosen priests and given them the greatest, most divine, and sublime power, so that whoever they bind on earth will also be bound in heaven.[11]

I earnestly implore all of you who are holy people and humble of heart. It is wrong to seek the favor of such men or to eat bread and drink with them.[12] Please do not even take alms from them until they repent weeping before God and release the servants of God and the baptized handmaids of Christ, the same ones he was crucified and died for.

Hear what scripture says:

- *The Most High rejects the gifts of the wicked. Whoever offers sacrifice from the goods of the poor is like someone who sacrifices a son before the eyes of his father.*[13]
- *The riches that a person earns unjustly will be vomited out of his belly. The angel of death will drag him away, the anger of dragons will torment him, the bite of the viper will kill him, and unquenchable fire will consume him.*[14]
- *Woe to those who fill themselves with that which is not their own.*[15]
- *What does it profit a man to gain the whole world but lose of his own soul?*[16]

It would take much too long to gather, list, and discuss a complete list of scriptures condemning such greed:

- *Greed is a deadly sin.*[17]
- *Do not desire the goods of your neighbor.*[18]
- *Do not murder.*[19]
- *No murderer can be with Christ.*[20]

- *Whoever hates his brother is counted as a murderer.*[21]
- *Whoever does not love his brother lives in death.*[22]

So how much worse is the man who stains his own hands with the blood of the children of God? These children are the very ones he recently acquired at the ends of the earth through me, though I am insignificant.

Did I come to Ireland without the help of God because I chose to? It was God who brought me here. I am bound by the Holy Spirit, so that I can't even see my own family.[23] Is it my own doing that I feel blessed mercy toward the very people who once enslaved me and killed so many male and female servants from my father's household? I am a freeborn man by the measure of this world and the son of a decurion.[24] But I sold my noble birth to serve others. I am not ashamed of this nor do I regret it. I am a slave of Christ for a foreign people for the sake of the indescribable glory of life everlasting which is in Christ Jesus our Lord.

So if my own people don't know me, then a prophet has no honor in his own country.[25] Maybe we're not all from the same flock and don't have the one God as our father. As scripture says: "Whoever is not with me is against me, and whoever does not gather with me scatters."[26]

It is wrong that one person builds and another destroys.[27] I am not seeking to do good for myself. I don't want to do my own will, but the will of God who has put this desire in me that I might be one of the hunters and fishermen that long ago he promised would come in the final days.[28]

These people hate me, but what can I do, O Lord? I am deeply despised. My God, see how your own sheep all about me are torn to pieces and driven away by these thieves—by the orders of this wicked Coroticus. Anyone who hands over Christians to the Irish and the Picts is far from God's love. They are savage wolves who have devoured the flock of God in Ireland that was growing so greatly by careful diligence.[29] I can't even count how many sons of the Irish and daughters of kings are becoming monks and virgins of Christ.

So let no evil deeds against the righteous please you, O God. Even hell will not be pleased.

Who among the Christian community would not recoil from laughing with such men or feasting with them? They decorate their homes with the spoils of dead Christians and live on plunder. These fools don't realize that the food they serve to friends and their own children is in fact deadly poison, just as Eve was ignorant that she handed over death to her own husband.[30] All who do evil deeds are like this. They work for their own punishment of everlasting death.

The Roman Christians in Gaul often send holy and worthy men to the Franks and other tribes with great bags of money to redeem baptized Christians who have been captured.[31] But you murder Christians and sell them to foreigners who don't even know God. It's as if you handed over the body of Christ to a house of prostitution.[32] What hope can you possibly have before God? Who will take your side or praise you? Indeed, God will judge you. As scripture says: "Not only those doing evil but even those condoning it will be damned."[33]

As for the murdered children of God cut down so bitterly by the sword, I don't know what more I can say. It is written that we should weep with those who weep and also that if one member of the body mourns we should all mourn.[34]

And the church also laments and grieves for her sons and daughters still alive but taken far away to a distant land where wickedness flourishes so abundantly, grievously, and shamelessly. In that land people born into freedom are sold and Christians are made into slaves of the most abominable, unworthy, and apostate Picts!

So I will raise my voice with sadness and grief:

> *O my beautiful and beloved brothers and children to whom I gave birth in Christ, so many that I cannot count you.*[35] *What can I do for you now? I am not worthy to help either God or men. The sins of the wicked have prevailed over us and we have been made like strangers from each other. Could it be they don't believe we have the same baptism or that we have one God as our father? They hate us because we are Irish. But scripture asks if you do not have one God and also why have you abandoned your neighbor?*[36]

So I mourn for you, my most beloved, I do mourn indeed. But I also rejoice inside myself. I have not worked among you in vain nor has my pilgrimage in Ireland been for nothing.[37] If this horrible, unspeakable crime did have to happen, I at least thank God that as baptized believers you have departed this world for paradise. I can see you even now as you begin your journey to that place where there will be no night, no sorrow, and no more death.[38] You will leap like calves released from their ropes[39]—and you will grind down the wicked so they will be like ashes under your feet.

You will rule with the apostles, the prophets, and martyrs and receive an everlasting kingdom. For Christ himself has said that believers will come from the east and the west and sit beside Abraham, Isaac, and Jacob in the kingdom of heaven, outside of which are dogs, sorcerers, and murderers.[40] Liars also and those who swear falsely will have their reward in a lake of everlasting fire.[41] For good reason the apostle says that if those who are just will barely be safe, where will sinners and ungodly breakers of the law find themselves?[42]

So as for Coroticus and his band of most evil criminals and rebels against Christ, where will they find themselves? They have distributed baptized Christian women as prizes, all for the sake of this fleeting world that will vanish in a moment. Like a cloud of smoke blown away by the wind, so these lying sinners will disappear from the sight of God.[43] But the righteous will feast in great happiness with Christ. They will judge the nations and rule over wicked kings forever and ever. Amen.

I, as ignorant as I am, declare before God and his angels that these things will happen just as God has revealed them to me. These are not my own words that I write in the Latin language, but those of God, the apostles, and prophets, who have never lied. Whoever believes this will be saved, but whoever does not will be condemned.[44] God has spoken.

I earnestly ask anyone who is God's servant to carry forth this letter, so that it will not be suppressed or hidden by anyone. Read it aloud before everyone and before Coroticus himself. May God inspire his men to come to their senses before him, so that, even though it is late, they might repent of their wicked crimes—these murderers of the brothers of the Lord—and release the baptized captives they stole away. In this way they still might earn the right to live with God and be saved, both in this world and for eternity.

Peace to the Father, the Son, and the Holy Spirit. Amen.

SAINT PATRICK'S CONFESSION

I am Patrick, a sinner and a very unsophisticated man. I am the least of all the faithful and to many the most despised.

My father's name was Calpornius.[1] He was a deacon[2] and his father was the priest[3] Potitus from the town of Bannaventa Berniae.[4] He owned a villa nearby, the place where I was captured when I was about sixteen years old. I didn't know the true God then. I was taken from there to Ireland with thousands of others. We deserved our fate because we had turned our backs on God and did not obey his commandments. We did not listen to our priests who warned us about our salvation. And the Lord overwhelmed us with the anger of his spirit and scattered us among many nations even to the very end of the earth.[5] Here my smallness is seen among strangers.

And in Ireland the Lord opened my understanding about my unbelief so that although it was late I might become aware of my sinful ways and turn with my whole heart to the Lord my

God.[6] He looked upon my misery and had mercy on my youth and ignorance. God watched over me before I knew him, before I had any wisdom, before I could distinguish between good and evil. He protected and comforted me as a father would his son.

Therefore I cannot be silent nor is it right for me to do so. I must tell of the great benefits and boundless grace the Lord granted me in the land of my captivity.

This is how we should give thanks to him. When he corrects us and we turn to him, we should lift him up and praise his wonders before every nation under heaven.

There is no other God.[7] There never was before nor will there be after except God the Father who is uncreated. He has no beginning himself, but in him all things have their beginning. He is indeed the one who rules over all.

Jesus Christ is his son. We profess that he was always present with the Father and spiritually begotten by the Father from before the beginning of the world, indeed before the beginning of anything, though how this happened is impossible to say. Through him all things were created, seen and unseen.[8] He became a man. After he conquered death, he was taken back to heaven by the Father. God has given him all power above every name in heaven and on earth and under the earth, so that every tongue will confess that Jesus Christ is Lord and God.[9] We believe in him and expect him to return soon to judge the living and the dead. He will reward each according to their deeds.[10]

He has abundantly poured upon us the Holy Spirit, the gift and promise of immortality.[11] He makes those who believe and obey into children of God and fellow heirs of Christ.

This is God whom we believe in and love—one God under the sacred name of the Trinity.

As he himself says through the prophet, "Call on me in your day of trouble and I will save you and you will glorify me."[12] And again he says, "It is honorable to make known and confess the works of God."[13]

Although I am far from perfect, I want my brothers and family to know what kind of person I am, so that they might understand the desires of my heart.

I am quite mindful of the words of my Lord, who declares in the psalm: "You will destroy those who speak lies."[14] And again he says, "The lying mouth destroys the soul."[15] And again the Lord says in the gospel, "On the day of judgment everyone will give an account of each idle word they have spoken."[16]

Therefore I ought to dread this judgment with fear and trembling on that day when no one will be able to escape or hide. All of us will give a reckoning of everything, even the smallest of sins, before the judgment seat of the Lord Christ.

Because of this I have long thought about writing this account, but I hesitated until now. I was afraid I would be criticized since I am not an educated man like those who have studied both law and scripture equally. Such men have not had to change their speech since they were boys, but have instead continually perfected it. I, on the other hand, have had to learn to speak in a foreign language.

You can easily see from my writing how limited my education has been. As it is written: "A wise man is known through his speech, as is understanding and knowledge and the teaching of truth."[17]

But what good is it to make excuses even if they are true? It's presumptuous for me as an old man to wish for something I failed to gain in my youth. My sins prevented me then from truly understanding what I had read.

But who will believe me if I repeat what I said before? I was only a young man, almost a speechless boy, when I was captured, before I knew what I ought to seek out or avoid. This is why today I am so embarrassed and am afraid to reveal my lack of learning. I'm not able to explain myself to educated men as clearly as my spirit and mind long to do so that my words might match my feelings. If only I had been given the same opportunity as others, then I would not be silent, hoping for my reward.

If some people think that I'm arrogant for speaking out in spite of my lack of education and poor language, remember what is written: "Stammering tongues will quickly learn to speak peace."[18] How much more we should desire this who are, as it is written, "the letter of Christ for salvation to the end of the earth."[19] And though not elegant, I am written in your hearts not with ink but with the spirit of the living God. Again the Spirit says, "Even the rustic man was created by the Most High."[20]

In my youth I was indeed a rustic, an ignorant exile who did not know how to look to the future. But this I know without a doubt—before I was humbled I was like a stone stuck deep in the mud. Then he who is powerful in his mercy lifted me up and raised me on high, placing me on top of a wall. Because of this I must proclaim blessings beyond human imagination with all my might and give thanks to the Lord for all his marvelous benefits, now and forever.

So be amazed all of you both great and small who fear God, all you wealthy and learned men. Listen to me and consider what I say. Who was it who raised me a fool, up from among you—all you who seem wise, learned in the law, powerful in speech and in every other way? Indeed it was God himself who inspired me, despised by this world, and put me ahead of others to serve faithfully throughout my life, if I am able, with fear and reverence, the people brought here and bought by Christ's love. He dedicated me to this task, if I am worthy to serve my people with true humility.

Since I believe in the Trinity, I must make known the gift of God and his eternal peace without fear of danger. I must faithfully spread the name of God everywhere, so that after I die I will leave an inheritance for my brothers and children, thousands of people, the ones I baptized in the Lord.

I was not worthy of what the Lord granted to me his servant after my enslavement after such great difficulties. After many years of slavery, he gave me abundant grace for the sake of these people. I never hoped for such a thing or even thought of it in my youth.

When I came to Ireland as a slave, I tended sheep daily and prayed frequently. My love for God grew more and more, and my fear of him as well, while my faith and spirit increased. In a single day I would pray a hundred times and the same at night, even when I was in the woods on the mountain. I rose before dawn to pray through snow or cold or rain. I suffered no harm from it and there was no laziness in me. I can see now that the spirit was burning inside me.

It was there one night while I was sleeping that I heard a voice speaking to me: "You have fasted well. Soon you will return home." Later I again heard a voice saying: "Behold, your ship is ready." But the ship was not nearby. It was perhaps two hundred miles away in a place I had never been nor did I know anyone there.[21] But soon after this I ran away and left the man I had served as a slave for six years. I traveled with courage from God, who guided my way toward good. I feared nothing—until I came to the ship.

On the day I arrived the ship was about to sail from that place. I asked if I could come with them, but the captain was angry and answered me harshly saying: "There is no way you are coming with us!" When I heard this I left him and walked back toward the hut where I was staying, praying as I went. But before my prayer was done I heard one of the sailors shouting at me: "Come back! We want to talk with you." I returned right away and they said to me, "Come, we'll take you on faith. Make a pact of friendship with us however you wish." But on that day I refused to suck their breasts because I feared God.[22] Still, since they were pagans, I did hope they would come to believe in Jesus Christ. So I had my way and we set out immediately.

Three days later we landed on the coast and wandered through an empty region for twenty-eight days.[23] They had no food and were starving, so that the next day the captain said to me: "Christian, what do you have to say? You claim your god is great and all-powerful. Why then are you unable to pray for us? We are worn down by hunger and it's not likely we'll ever see living souls again."

But confidently I said to them: "Turn your hearts in faith to the Lord my God, for nothing is impossible to him. From his abundance he may send food to you this very day on your journey so that you will be satisfied."

And with God's help, that's exactly what happened. Suddenly a herd of pigs appeared before us on the road. They killed many of them and their hunger was satisfied. They stayed there for two nights and even their dogs were full, as many of them had grown very weak and were barely alive by that point.[24] After this they gave thanks to God and I was honored in their eyes, for from that day on they had abundant food. They even found some wild honey and gave me part of it, with one of them saying, "This has been offered as a sacrifice." Thanks be to God, I had eaten none of it.[25]

Then while I was sleeping that very night, Satan greatly tempted me. I will remember the experience as long as I am in this body. Something like a huge rock seemed to fall on me so that I couldn't move my arms or legs. How did it come to my mind, ignorant about spiritual matters, to call on Elijah? Just at the point I saw the sun rising in the sky, I called out, "Elijah, Elijah" with all my strength. Behold, the rays of the sun fell on me and suddenly took away the weight off my limbs.[26] I believe it was Christ Jesus himself helping me and his Spirit crying out through me. I hope it will be the same way on the day of my distress. As the gospel says, "On that day," the Lord declares, "it is not you who speaks but the Spirit of your Father who speaks in you."[27]

Many years later, I was once again captured. During the first night I was with them I heard a divine voice speaking to me saying, "For two months you will be with them." And that's exactly what happened. On the sixtieth night the Lord freed me from their hands.

But on this previous journey, God looked after us with food, fire, and dry weather each day until on the tenth day we reached a village. As I said above, we traveled through a deserted region for twenty-eight days, then ran out of food on the same night we arrived at the settlement.

And so after a few years I was again with my parents in Britain. They welcomed me home as their son and begged me never to leave them again after all the difficulties I had been through.

It was there I saw a vision during the night of a man coming as if from Ireland.[28] Victoricus was his name and he carried many letters with him.[29] He gave me one of them and I read the beginning which said: "The Voice of the Irish." While I was reading this I thought I heard the voice of those who dwell beside the wood of Voclut near the western sea.[30] It was as if they were crying out with a single voice: "Holy boy, we beg you, come back and walk among us again."[31] I was struck through my heart and could read no more, then I awoke. I thank God that after many years the Lord granted them their request.

Then on another night—whether it happened inside me or near me I don't know, God knows[32]—I heard words clearly spoken but that I could not understand, except those at the end saying: "He who gave his life for you, he himself speaks in you." I awoke full of joy.

At another time I saw someone praying inside me as if I were within my own body. I heard him praying above me—that is, above the inner man[33]—and he was praying powerfully with sighs. All through this I was confused and astonished and wondered who it was who was praying inside me. But at the end of the prayer he said that he was the Spirit. I woke up then and remembered what the apostle said: "The Spirit helps the weakness in our prayers. For we do not know what we should pray for, but the Spirit himself prays for us with unspeakable sighs that cannot be expressed in words."[34] And again: "The Lord our advocate speaks for us."[35]

When I was accused by some of my superiors who came forward and accused me of sins contrary to my work as a bishop, on that day I was struck down mightily and might have fallen in this life and for eternity. But the Lord kindly showed mercy to a stranger and pilgrim on account of his own name and helped me greatly in my affliction so that I did not slip into shame and infamy. I pray that God does not hold this sin against them.

The charge they brought against me after thirty years was because of a confession I had made before I was even a deacon. In those days I was anxious and worried and I told my best friend about something I had done in my youth one day, even in an hour, because I was then still weak. I don't know, God knows, perhaps I was only fifteen at the time. I didn't believe in the living God then—I hadn't since childhood—but remained in death and unbelief until I was severely punished, and truly brought low by hunger and nakedness every day.

I didn't go to Ireland of my own free will. Indeed I almost died there. But it turned out well for me since I was chastised by the Lord. God made me what I am today, someone far different than I was then, so that I might work for the care and salvation of others. At that time I didn't even care about myself.

On the day mentioned above when those churchmen rejected me, I saw a vision during that same night. There were shameful letters written opposite my face and all at once I heard a divine voice saying to me: "We have seen with anger the face of our chosen one stripped of honor." Note that the voice did not say, "*You* have seen with anger," but "*We* have seen with anger," as if he were joined to me. As it is written: "Whoever touches you, touches the apple of my eye."[36]

I therefore give thanks to him who comforts me in everything, for he did not hinder me in the journey I chose and in the work that I had learned from Christ the Lord. But instead I felt a great strength within myself and knew my faith was established before God and men alike.

So I boldly declare to you all that my conscience is clear now and for all time. With God as my witness, I have not lied to you.

But I do feel sorry that we had to hear such words from my dear friend, the one I had trusted with the secret of my soul. I wasn't present at the meeting nor was I in Britain nor did I request the meeting, but I did learn from some of the brothers before the hearing that he would speak up for me in my absence. He had even once told me with his own lips: "Behold, you are going to be given the rank of bishop"—though I was not worthy. But why then later did he disgrace me in front of all those people, good and bad alike, about something he had in the past gladly and freely pardoned, as has the Lord who is greater than everyone?

I have said enough about this. But I must not conceal the gift of God that he has given to me in the land of my captivity, because I earnestly sought him out and there I found him and he saved me from all evil. I believe this because his Spirit lives inside me and has worked in me up to this very day. Again, I know I'm speaking boldly, but God knows that if a mere mortal had said these things to me perhaps I would have remained silent because of Christ's love.

And so I offer tireless thanks to my God who preserved his faithful one in the day of my temptation so that now I can confidently offer a sacrifice to him, by which I mean the living sacrifice of my soul to Christ my Lord.[37] He saved me in all my troubles so that I can ask "Lord, who am I?" and "What is my calling?"

With such divine power you saved me so that now I can praise and glorify your name always among the pagans wherever I am, both in my success and in my failure. Whatever happens to me, good or bad, I must always give thanks to God who has shown me that I can trust in him without limit. He is the one who heard me, an ignorant man, in these final days so that I might dare to take up this most noble and holy work. I am among those men the Lord said would come when his gospel would be preached as a witness to all nations before the end of the world. We now have seen these words are fulfilled. Behold, we are witnesses that the gospel has been preached to the edge of the inhabited world.

It would take me too long to tell the whole story of my work in whole or part of it. I will simply say that God, who is most merciful, often freed me from slavery and from twelve dangers which threatened my life. Aside from these there were many other betrayals I don't wish to describe in detail, for I don't wish to bore my readers. But God, who knows all things before they happen, frequently gave me warnings, unworthy man that I am, through divine revelations.

Where did such wisdom come from? It wasn't from within me, for I didn't know the number of my days nor did I understand God. But where did I get that wondrous, life-giving gift that I might know and love God, though I had to leave my home and parents to do it?

Many people offered me gifts with weeping and tears. I offended the givers of these donations contrary to the wishes of some of my superiors. But with God guiding me, I would not go along with them or consent to these gifts in any way. This was not by my grace but by God who is strong within me and resists them all. I did this so that I might come to the Irish pagans to preach the gospel and suffer insults from unbelievers, so that I might hear reproach because of my wanderings and suffer many persecutions, including being placed in chains, while I sacrifice my free birth for the good of others. If I am worthy, I am even ready to give up my life freely and without hesitation for the sake of his name. It is in Ireland I wish to live out my life to the end, if the Lord will grant my prayer.

I am in great debt to God, who gave me such grace so that many people have been reborn in him and then brought to completion. Clergy have also been ordained for these people who are just now coming to the faith, the ones the Lord has brought to himself from the ends of the earth. As he said through his prophets: "The gentiles shall come to you from the ends of the earth saying, 'How false are the idols of our fathers, for there is no profit in them.'"[38] And again scripture says: "I have placed you as a light among the gentiles that you might bring salvation to the end of the earth."[39]

And there I wish to await the promise of him who does not ever deceive us. As he promises in the gospel: "They will come from the east and west to recline at the table of Abraham, Isaac, and Jacob."[40] So we trust that believers will come from all the earth.

So it is proper for us to fish well and diligently, as the Lord warns and teaches us saying: "Follow me and I will make you fishers of men."[41] And again he says through the prophets: "Behold, I send forth many fishermen and hunters," and so forth.[42] Thus we ought to cast our nets with boldness to catch a great many for God and to assure that there are clergy everywhere to baptize and preach to a people hungry and needy.

The Lord says in the gospel when he warns and teaches saying: "Go therefore now and teach all people baptizing them in the name of the Father and the Son and the Holy Spirit, teaching them to observe all that I have taught you. And behold I am with you each day until the end of the age."[43] And again he says: "Going therefore into the whole world, preach the gospel to every creature. Whoever believes and is baptized will be saved, but whoever does not believe will be condemned."[44] And again: "This gospel of the kingdom will be preached in the whole world as a testimony to all nations, and then the end will come."[45] And again the Lord spoke through the prophet saying: "There will be in the final days, says the Lord, a pouring forth of my spirit over all flesh, so that your sons and your daughters will prophesy, and your young men will see visions and your old men dream dreams. Indeed in those days I will pour out my spirit on my male and female servants and they will prophesy."[46] And the prophet Hosea says: "I will call 'my people' those who are not my people, and I will call 'beloved' she who is not my beloved. And in the very place it was said to them that you are not my people, there they will be called the sons of the living God."[47]

How is it that the Irish who never had any knowledge of God, worshipping only idols and unclean things, have now become a people of the Lord and are called sons of God? The sons of the Irish and daughters of kings are even becoming monks and virgins of Christ.

Indeed there was a blessed and very beautiful Irish woman of the nobility that I had baptized, who came to us after a few days for this very reason. She said she had received a divine summons from an angel of God to become a virgin of Christ and so draw closer to God. Thanks be to God, six days later she did what was worthy of praise and earnestly embraced the life that all virgins of God choose.

The fathers of these women don't approve of this and the women suffer maltreatment and false accusations from their parents, but still their numbers continue to grow.

We don't know how many have embraced the celibate life in Ireland by our efforts, not including those widows and women who practice celibacy in marriage. But it's the slave women who suffer most. They are subject to constant harassment and terror. But the Lord gives grace to his many handmaidens, for even though they are forbidden to follow him they bravely imitate the Lord.

So even if I wished to leave these women and go to Britain—and I was quite ready to visit my country and family and to travel on to Gaul to visit the brothers and see the face of the Lord's saints—I wanted that very much, God knows. Nevertheless I am bound by the Holy Spirit who declares that if I left I would be guilty of sin. I'm afraid of abandoning the work I've begun here. No, not my work, but that of Christ the Lord who has ordered me to stay with these people for the rest of my life, if the Lord is willing and will save me from every evil path so that I may not sin before him.

But I hope that I have done well, though I don't trust myself as long as I am trapped in this body of death.[48] For he is strong who tries daily to turn me away from my faith and the pure chastity that I have chosen to embrace to the end of my life for Christ my Lord. But the hostile flesh always drags me toward death, to those enticing, forbidden desires.

I know that I have certainly not led a perfect life like other believers. I confess this to my Lord and am not ashamed in his sight. I am not lying.[49] Since I first came to know the Lord when I was a young man, the love of God and the fear of him have grown in me, so that by the Lord's grace I have kept the faith until this day.[50]

Let whoever wants to laugh go ahead and mock me, but I will not be silent nor will I hide the signs and wonders which were shown to me by the Lord years before they happened. For God knows everything from before the beginning of the world.

I should give thanks without ceasing to God who so often forgave my foolishness and carelessness. On many more occasions he did not show his anger against me, I the one who had been chosen as his helper, though a helper slow to do what he revealed to me—as the Holy Spirit reminded me. The Lord showed mercy to me a thousand thousand times because he looked inside me and saw that although I was ready, I didn't know what to do because of my confused state.

There were many people who tried to prevent my mission to Ireland. They would talk behind my back and say: "Why does this man put himself in danger among those barbarians who do not know God?" I can testify that they didn't do this out of malice, but because they honestly didn't believe that someone as rustic as me—and I admit that I am—could carry out such a task. I wasn't quick to recognize then the grace that was within me, as I now know I should have.

So now I have given a straightforward account to my brothers and fellow servants who have believed me on account of what I said and say still so that I might strengthen and confirm your faith. I earnestly hope that you will strive for greater things and perform better deeds than I have done. This will be my reward, for "a wise son is the glory of his father."[51]

You all know, as does God, that I have lived among you since my youth in genuine faith and sincerity of heart. Likewise I have been faithful among the pagans with whom I now live and will continue to be so. God knows that I have taken advantage of no one. For the sake of God and his church I would never do so because I might provoke persecution of them and all of us. I also wouldn't do so because I wouldn't have the name of the Lord sullied because of me. As it is written: "Woe to the one through whom the name of the Lord is blasphemed."[52]

Even though I'm imperfect in all things, nonetheless I have tried to preserve myself for the sake of my Christian brothers and the virgins of Christ and the religious women who on their own used to give me small donations and place some of their jewelry on the altar. I returned these gifts, though they were offended. But I did so in hope of lasting success, so that I might carefully preserve my work for the long term. I didn't wish to give nonbelievers any chance to complain about me or criticize my holy work. Not even in the smallest matter would I give them the opportunity to speak against me or my character.

When I baptized thousands of converts, did I ever expect even a small token from them in return? If so, tell me and I will repay you.[53] Or when the Lord ordained clergy everywhere through my unworthiness and when I gave my ministry to them for free, if I asked anyone even for the price of my shoes, witness against me and I will repay you.

On the contrary, I spent myself for you all so that they would receive me. I traveled among you everywhere risking many dangers for your sake even to the farthest places beyond which no one lived. No one had ever gone that far to baptize or ordain clergy or serve the people. With the help of God, I did this with great care and most gladly for your salvation.

I admit that on occasion I did give gifts to kings, in addition to the money I gave their sons who traveled with me. Even so, one time they detained me and my companions and very much wanted to kill me, though my time had not yet come. They took everything of value that we carried and put me in chains. But after two weeks the Lord freed me from their power and they returned everything they had stolen. For this I owed thanks to God and to some good friends we had seen earlier.

You all know how much I paid the judges in all those places I frequently visited. I must have paid them the price of fifteen men so that you might enjoy my company and I might always enjoy yours in God. I don't regret it nor do I intend to stop. I'm still spending now and will spend more. The Lord is powerful. May he grant me that I may spend my very self for your souls.

Listen to me. I call on God as my witness upon my soul that I am telling you the truth. I don't write this to you as a tale of flattery or greed. Nor do I write because I am seeking any honor from you. The honor that is unseen but dwells in the heart is enough for me. For he who promised is faithful. He never lies.

I see now that in this present age I have been highly exalted by the Lord. I am not worthy of this nor am I the sort of person he should have honored. I know very well that I am better suited to poverty and calamity than riches and pleasures. But even as Christ was made poor for our sake, so too I am made wretched and unfortunate.

I have no wealth even if I did want it. I am not judging myself. Every day I expect to be murdered, kidnapped, made a slave, or something else. But I am not afraid of any of these things because of the promises of heaven. I have placed myself in the hands of almighty God who rules everywhere. As the prophet says, "Cast your burden on God and he will sustain you."[54]

Behold, I entrust my spirit to my most faithful God whose ambassador I am, though I am not worthy. Because God does not play favorites, he chose me for this task so that I might be one of the least of his servants.

I will give back what is due to him because of all that he has done for me. But what can I say or give my Lord since everything I have is a gift from him? It's enough that he searches the heart and innermost parts and knows that I was willing to drink the cup he had prepared for me, just as he gave it to the others who loved him.[55]

So may my God never separate me from the people he has bought for himself at the ends of the earth. I pray to God that he give me perseverance and allow me to remain a faithful witness to him until the end of my life for his sake.

If I have ever done anything good for the sake of my God that I love, I ask of him that I might be able to shed my blood with those converts and captives for the sake of his name, even if it means I will not be granted a grave or that my poor body will be torn apart by dogs or wild animals or devoured by the birds of the air. I firmly believe that if this should happen to me, I will have gained my soul as well as my body. For without a doubt we shall rise again on that day in the brightness of the sun which is the glory of Jesus

Christ our redeemer. We will be sons of the living God and fellow heirs with Christ, conformed to his image.[56] For we shall rule from him, through him, and in him.

The sun we see rises for us each day by God's command, but it will never rule nor will its splendor last. Those who worship it will come into terrible punishment. But we believe in and adore the true sun, Christ, who will never perish. Neither will those perish who do his will, but they will live forever just as Christ lives forever. Christ has reigned with God the Father almighty and with the Holy Spirit since before time and for now and for all time to come. Amen.

And so I briefly state my declaration again—I testify truly and with joy in my heart before God and his holy angels that I have had no purpose in returning to the Irish, from whom I once escaped, except to preach the gospel and the promises of God.

I do pray that any of you who believe in God and fear him— whoever you might be who comes upon these words written in Ireland by Patrick the ignorant sinner—that none of you will say that in my ignorance I did anything worthy, but that you might realize and truly believe that any small thing I accomplished or did that was pleasing to God was done through his gift.

This is my declaration before I die.

THE FIRST SYNOD
OF SAINT PATRICK

A synod in the early Christian church was a gathering of bishops in council to rule on theological and practical issues facing the members of their communities. The rulings from one such council form what is known as the *First Synod of Saint Patrick*, the earliest list of official church decisions we possess from Ireland. Although the rules are ascribed to Patrick along with the bishops Auxilius and Iserninus, it is probably not from Patrick's own lifetime. Nonetheless, the *First Synod,* as seen from many of the issues it addresses, does come from an early age when druids and other non-Christians were still prevalent on the island.

The rulings are divided into those dealing with the clergy and those dealing with Christians in general. The importance of ecclesiastical jurisdiction is stressed repeatedly, with clergy being warned not to preach or collect alms outside their allotted sphere of authority. The laity in turn are repeatedly cautioned in their dealings with pagans.

The *First Synod* is a short document but an invaluable source of information about the practical workings of the church and its members in the earliest days of Irish Christianity.

Two full Latin editions with translations and helpful notes are Ludwig Bieler, *The Irish Penitentials,* 54–59, 240; and M. J. Faris, ed., *The Bishops' Synod.* Bieler also presents a translation with notes in *The Works of St. Patrick*, 50–54, 96–99.

Here begins the synod of the bishops Patrick, Auxilius, and Iserninus.[1]

We give thanks to God the Father and the Son and the Holy Spirit. The bishops Patrick, Auxilius, and Iserninus send greetings to priests and deacons and to every member of the clergy.

To us it seems better to warn the careless beforehand rather than blame them for their actions later. As Solomon says, "It is better to reason than be angry."[2]

Copies of our decisions have been recorded and are given below.

1. If anyone in his own community on his own authority and without permission has attempted to ransom captives, he deserves to be excommunicated.
2. Lectors should become familiar with the church in which they sing the psalms.[3]
3. There shall be no wandering cleric in the community.
4. If anyone has received permission to collect money and has done so, he shall not receive more than necessary.

5. If any money remains, he shall put it on the bishop's altar so that it may be given to another needy person.

6. Any clergyman, from porter[4] to priest, who is seen without a tunic and does not cover the shame of his belly and his nakedness or if he has not cut his hair in the Roman manner[5] or if his wife has gone about with her hair unveiled, then let them be held in contempt by the laity and excommunicated from the church.

7. Any clergyman who when summoned does not come to morning or evening prayers because of neglect shall be considered a stranger, unless he is detained by the yoke of slavery.

8. If a clergyman has given a pledge for a pagan in any amount and if, as is not surprising, that pagan cheats him using some trick, the clergyman shall pay what is owed from his own resources. If the clergyman resorts to armed combat with the pagan, he shall with just cause be considered excommunicated from the church.

9. A monk and a virgin—he from one place and she from another—shall not stay together in the same guest house, nor shall they travel from one town to another in the same vehicle, nor shall they carry on long conversations.

10. If any man has made a good beginning singing psalms but then quits and lets his hair grow, he shall be excommunicated from the church until he returns to his former state.

11. If any clergyman has been excommunicated by someone and another receives him, both must do the same penance.

12. If any Christian has been excommunicated, his alms shall not be accepted.

13. Alms from pagans shall not be accepted by the church.

14. A Christian who has committed murder or fornication or, in the manner of the pagans, has sworn before a soothsayer,[6] shall spend a year in penance for each offense. When the year is complete, he shall come with witnesses and be absolved by a priest.

15. He who has committed theft shall do penance for half a year, with twenty of these days on bread, and, if possible, return the stolen goods. Then he shall be restored to the church.

16. Any Christian who believes there is such a thing as a *lamia*[7] in this world—that is, a vampire[8]—is to be excommunicated for giving a living soul that reputation. He shall not be received back into the church until he has publically recanted the charge he has made and done penance with all diligence.

17. A virgin who has vowed to God to remain chaste and afterward marries a spouse in the flesh is to be excommunicated until she changes her ways. If she repents and sends away the adulterer, she shall do penance and not live in the same household or settlement as him.

18. If someone is excommunicated, he shall not enter the church even on Easter night until he accepts penance.

19. A Christian woman who takes a man in honorable marriage and then deserts her husband to join with another in adultery shall be excommunicated.

20. A Christian who does not pay a debt, just like a pagan, shall be excommunicated until he pays what he owes.

21. If a Christian is wronged by someone and calls that person into court to hear the case instead of before the church, that man shall be considered a stranger.

22. If anyone gives his daughter in proper marriage to a man, then she loves another with her father agreeing and accepting a bride price, both shall be excommunicated from the church.[9]

23. If any priest has built a church, he may not offer mass there until his bishop consecrates it, as is right.

24. If a newcomer comes to a community he shall not baptize, nor offer mass, nor consecrate, nor build a church until he has permission from the bishop. For whoever seeks permission from pagans shall be a stranger.

25. If an offering is given by pious people on days when the bishop is in residence at a church, the offering shall be considered a pontifical gift, as is the ancient custom, and the bishop may keep it for himself or distribute it to the needy as he sees fit.

26. But if a cleric disobeys and is caught using some of the gifts, he shall be excommunicated from the church for his shameful greed.

27. Any clergyman who comes into the community of a bishop shall not baptize or offer mass or perform any duties. If he does not obey this rule, he shall be excommunicated.

28. If any cleric has been excommunicated, he shall pray alone and not in the same house as the brothers. He is not allowed

to say mass or consecrate until he has made amends. If he does not do so, he shall be doubly punished.

29. If one of the brothers wishes to receive the grace of God, he shall not be baptized until he has fasted forty days.

30. Any bishop who goes out from his own jurisdiction to another's shall not presume to ordain unless he has received permission from him who holds jurisdiction in the place. On Sunday he shall offer mass only if invited and he shall be content in obedience.

31. If one of two clergymen who are at odds over some matter hires an enemy of the other to kill him, he is a murderer. Such a clergyman is to be considered a stranger by all righteous people.

32. If any clergyman wishes to help a captive, he shall do so with his own money. For if he takes that captive away, many clergymen will be blamed because of one thief. Whoever does this shall be excommunicated.

33. Any clergyman who comes from the Britons without a letter, even if he lives in the community, is not allowed to serve.

34. Similarly, if one of our deacons goes to a different community without a letter and without permission from his abbot, he should not be given food and he shall be punished by the priest he has disobeyed. Also a monk who wanders without the permission of his abbot shall be punished.

The end of the statutes of the synod.

THE HYMN OF SAINT SECUNDINUS

The Irish annals record that Secundinus—Sechnall in Irish— was a missionary who joined Patrick in Ireland in 439 and died eight years later. Other documents say that he was one of Patrick's bishops, who founded a church at Dunshaughlin in County Meath and composed the hymn below. Whatever the merits of these accounts, the hymn listed under his name is one of the earliest examples of the literature and legend that grew up around the cult of Saint Patrick.

The hymn is lavish in praise of its hero and allows none of the self-doubt and shortcomings Patrick reveals in his own letters. It is composed of twenty-three stanzas in what is known as an abecedarian arrangement, each stanza in the original Latin beginning with a consecutive letter of the alphabet. Thus the initial word of the first stanza is *Audite* ("listen"), that of the second stanza *Beata* ("blessed"), and so forth to *Zona* ("belt"). This abecedarian style is found in several of the biblical psalms (e.g., Psalm 119) and in hymns by Augustine and other early Christian authors.

At the end of his *Life of Saint Patrick*, Muirchú states that "whoever sings the hymn composed about you on the day of his death will have his penance for sins determined" by Patrick, a likely reference to this same hymn.

The Latin text with linguistic notes is presented in Ludwig Bieler, "The Hymn of St. Secundinus." His translation and additional notes are in *The Works of St. Patrick*, 57–65, 100–103. Andy Orchard provides a translation and presents an argument for the literary merits of the hymn in Dumville (ed.), *Saint Patrick:* A.D. 493–1993, 153–173.

Listen, all of you who love God, to the holy merits
of the bishop Patrick, a man blessed in Christ.
Because of his excellent ways he is like unto the angels,
and because of his perfect life he is the equal of the apostles.

He keeps in every way the blessed teachings of Christ.
His deeds shine brightly among the people,
those who follow his holy and wondrous example,
and thus praise the Father and Lord in the heavens.

He is constant in his fear of God and unshakable in his faith.
On him the church is built, as on Peter.[1]

He has received his apostleship from God.
The gates of hell will not prevail against him.

The Lord has chosen him to instruct the barbarians
and to fish with the nets of doctrine.[2]
From the world he draws believers to grace,
those who would follow the Lord to his heavenly seat.

He sells the chosen talents of the gospel of Christ
which he collects with interest among the Irish pagans.
As a reward for his labor on his journey,
he will have the joy of the kingdom of heaven with Christ.

A faithful minister of God and his distinguished messenger,
he brings to good people the model and example of the apostles.
He preaches to the people of God in word and deed,
so that the one not transformed by his words is moved by his actions.

He has glory with Christ and honor in this age.
He is venerated by all as an angel of God,
whom God sent, as he did Paul, an apostle to the gentiles,
so that he might guide them to the kingdom of God.

He is humble in spirit and body because of the fear of God,
and the Lord delights in him because of his good deeds.
He bears the holy marks of Christ on his body.
The glory of the cross alone sustains him.

He feeds believers diligently with the heavenly banquet,
so that those who are seen with Christ will not faint on the journey.
He gives to them as bread the words of the gospel,
in his hands they are multiplied like manna.[3]

He keeps his body pure because of his love for God,
a body he has prepared as a temple for the Holy Spirit,
the one who constantly imbues him with pure actions,
deeds he offers as a living sacrifice pleasing to the Lord.

He is the light of the world,[4] *the shining one of the gospel,*
raised up on a candlestick, shining out on the whole world.
He is the fixed city of the king on a mountaintop,
which possesses great abundance of the Lord.

He will be called the greatest in the kingdom of God
who fulfills with good deeds the holy words he preaches.
He puts forth by his good example the essence of the faithful
and in a pure heart he has confidence in God.

He boldly proclaims the name of the Lord to the pagans
and gives them eternal grace with the baptism of salvation.
He prays to God daily for their sins,
for them he offers sacrifices worthy to God.

For the glory of God he spurns all the riches of this world,
all such things he ranks as nothing compared to the table of God.

The violent clashes of this world do not move him.
Suffering for Christ, he rejoices in adversity.

He is a good and faithful shepherd of gospel's flock.
God has chosen him to guard his people
and to feed them with divine teaching,
people for whom he gives his life, according to the example of Christ.

The savior has raised him to the office of bishop because of his merits,
so that he trains clerics as a heavenly army,
giving them heavenly nourishment along with their vestments,
which are covered by divine and sacred words.

He is the messenger of the king who invites believers to the wedding.[5]
He is richly clothed in the wedding garment.
He drinks celestial wine from heavenly vessels
and gives the people of God a spiritual cup.

He finds a holy treasure in the sacred book,
sees the divinity in the flesh of the savior,
this treasure he buys with holy and righteous works.
"Israel" his soul is called, for he sees God.[6]

He is a faithful witness of the Lord to the universal law.
His words are sprinkled with divine oracles,
so that human flesh will not decay, eaten by worms,
but salted with celestial flavor for sacrifice.[7]

He is a true and famous farmer of the gospel's fields.[8]
His seeds are seen as the gospel of Christ.
He sows them from his divine mouth into the ears of the wise,
whose hearts and minds he plows with the Holy Spirit.

Christ chose him to be his representative on earth.
He frees captives from a double bondage,
redeeming many from human servitude
and liberating countless people from the rule of the devil.

He sings hymns, and the Apocalypse,[9] *and the psalms of God,*
he explains them for the edification of the people of God.
He believes in the law of the sacred Trinity
and teaches that in three persons there is but a single substance.

He girds himself with the belt of the Lord day and night.
He prays to the Lord God without ceasing.[10]
He will receive the reward of his great labors,
when he, holy, rules over Israel with the apostles.[11]

"SAINT PATRICK'S BREASTPLATE"

The "Breastplate" is one of the most famous and beloved works of early Irish Christianity. Although it is doubtful that Patrick composed the piece, it has long been associated with him. The title is a translation from the Latin term *lorica* and evokes a military image of arming oneself found in the Apostle Paul's first New Testament letter to the Thessalonians (5.8): "Put on the breastplate of faith and love, and the helmet of hope for salvation." It is not alone as an early Irish prayer of protection, with similar surviving examples attributed to holy men such as Gildas, Sanctán, and Mael Ísu.

The preface, written at a later time, refers to an episode found in Muirchú's *Life of Saint Patrick* in which Patrick escaped an ambush laid by Loíguire, the Irish high king, by turning himself and his companions into deer. The alternate title of "The Deer's Cry" (*Fáeth Fiada* in Old Irish) is supposedly based on this encounter, but it may come from a term which originally referred to a druidic spell of invisibility.

What is most striking about the "Breastplate" is its powerful use of language and imagery, most effective when the prayer is read aloud. The translation tries to capture the driving sense of the original Old Irish, which, although not poetry, is composed in alliterative, rhythmical prose:

> Atomriug indiu
>> niurt Dé dom lúamairecht
>> cumachtae nDé dom chumgabail
>> cíall Dé dom imthús
>
> *I rise today,*
>> *with the strength of God to lead me,*
>> *with the power of God to lift me,*
>> *with the wisdom of God to guide me.*

From the beginning, the prayer evokes the power of God to protect those who recite it against troubles and dangers, calling on Christ, the host of heaven, and nature itself to guard against all manner of evil. Such dangers include the snares of the devil, temptations of the flesh, and, notably, the magic spells of women, blacksmiths, and druids. The final arming of oneself with Christ is followed by a rousing conclusion repeating the first stanza of the prayer—declaring that the supplicant is now fully prepared for the challenges of the day ahead.

The Old Irish text with translation is found in Whitley Stokes and John Strachan, eds., *Thesaurus Paleohibernicus*, vol. 2, 354–358. A translation with notes is in Ludwig Bieler, *The Works of St. Patrick*,

67–72, 104–105. Notes on this invocation and similar prayers can be found in James Kenney, *The Sources for the Early History of Ireland,* 270–274.

This hymn was written by Patrick. It was composed in the time of Loíguire son of Niall.[1] The occasion for its composition was to protect Patrick and his monks against the deadly perils that these clergymen faced.

This is a breastplate of faith for protection of body and soul against demons, men, and evils. If anyone will repeat it every day with diligence to God, demons will not dare to confront him. It will protect him against all poisons and envy. It will be a protection for him against sudden death and a breastplate for his soul after death.

Patrick sang this hymn when Loíguire prepared an ambush for him to prevent him from going to Tara[2] and sowing the faith. They seemed as wild deer with a fawn, that is, Benén,[3] following behind them, to those lying in wait for them.

The name of the prayer is "The Deer's Cry":

I rise today
>   *with a mighty strength, an invocation of the Trinity,*
>   *believing in the threeness,*
>   *confessing the oneness,*
>   *of the creator of creation.*

I rise today

> *through the strength of Christ with his baptism,*
> *through the strength of his crucifixion with his burial,*
> *through the strength of his resurrection and his ascension,*
> *through the strength of his return for the final judgment.*

I rise today

> *through the strength of the love of the cherubim,*[4]
> *in the obedience of angels,*
> *in the service of archangels,*
> *in hope of the resurrection to gain reward,*
> *in the prayers of the patriarchs,*[5]
> *in the foretellings of the prophets,*
> *in the preaching of the apostles,*
> *in the faith of the confessors,*[6]
> *in the purity of holy virgins,*
> *in the deeds of righteous men.*

I rise today

> *through the strength of the sky,*
> *through the radiance of the sun,*
> *through the light of the moon,*
> *through the brilliance of fire,*
> *through the speed of lightning,*
> *through the swiftness of the wind,*
> *through the depth of the sea,*
> *through the steadiness of earth,*
> *through the firmness of rock.*

I rise today,

> *with the strength of God to lead me,*
> *with the power of God to lift me,*
> *with the wisdom of God to guide me,*
> *with the eye of God to see before me,*
> *with the ear of God to listen for me,*
> *with the word of God to speak for me,*
> *with the hand of God to guard me,*
> *with the path of God to stretch before me,*
> *with the shield of God to protect me,*
> *with the army of God to stand before me,*
>> *against the snares of demons,*
>> *against the temptations of sin,*
>> *against the weakness of my nature,*
>> *against all who wish me ill,*
>>> *whether I am far or near,*
>>> *alone or in a crowd.*

I call today on all these powers to protect me,
> *from the cruel and merciless forces that might attack my body and soul,*
> *from the incantations of false prophets,*
> *from the dark magic of pagans,*
> *from the misleading ways of heretics,*
> *from the snares of idolatry,*
> *from the spells of women,[7] blacksmiths,[8] and druids,[9]*
> *from all that attacks body and soul.*
> *Christ protect me today,*

from poison and fire,
from water and wounds,
so that I may gain my fullness of rewards.
Christ beside me, Christ before me, Christ behind me,
Christ within me, Christ beneath me, Christ above me,
Christ on my right, Christ on my left,
Christ in breadth, Christ in length, Christ in height,
Christ in the heart of everyone who thinks of me,
Christ in the mouth of everyone who speaks of me,
Christ in every eye that sees me,
Christ in every ear that hears me.

I rise today
with a mighty strength, an invocation of the Trinity,
believing in the threeness,
confessing the oneness,
of the creator of creation.

MUIRCHÚ'S *LIFE OF SAINT PATRICK*

We know little about the life of Muirchú except that he was an Irish churchman who lived and wrote in the late seventh century, two hundred years after the death of Patrick. In his *Life of Saint Patrick*, he asserts that he is following (in a presumably spiritual sense) in the footsteps of his father Cogitosus, the author of the *Life of Saint Brigid* found later in this volume. Muirchú addresses his work to Áed, bishop of Sleaty, who died about 700. Along with Áed, Muirchú attended the Synod of Birr in 697 and was a signatory there to the law of Adamnán, which urged protection for women and children in times of war. Muirchú may well have been a churchman from Armagh, but whatever his origins he was, along with his contemporary Tírechán, among the first to transform the life of Patrick into a spiritual biography.

Telling the story of the life of a Christian saint is known as *hagiography*, from the Greek *hagios* ("holy") and *graphe* ("writing"). The genre can trace its roots back to classical biographies, notably those by Plutarch and other writers who were concerned as much or more with providing a moral lesson to their readers as they were with recording history. Lives of worthy Christians were likewise told from the beginning of the religion. Indeed, the gospels themselves could be considered the primary model for early hagiography. But it was the rise of monasticism in the fourth century that led communities to celebrate their founders by writing stories of their lives. Monasteries became centers of hagiographical writing where the lives of holy men and women were remembered and celebrated.

The fourth-century *Life of Anthony* of Egypt written by Athanasius, bishop of Alexandria, is one of the earliest and most influential examples of the genre. Lives and legends of monks and the miracles they performed were collected and edited frequently in the following centuries. The later *Life of Martin of Tours* by Sulpicius Severus became a model for many western hagiographical accounts and was a widely circulated work in Ireland. The *Life* tells Martin's story as a soldier who becomes a Christian and turns his back on the world to follow God in seclusion as a monk, though he later becomes a bishop. Martin heals the sick, raises the dead, demolishes pagan temples, and fights the temptations of the devil. But most important, he serves as an example of piety for all believers.

Hagiography was never intended to be a historical description of a subject's life as much as an inspiration for Christians in their own spiritual journey. Or, as Athanasius says to his readers in the preface to his *Life of Anthony*, "so that you might lead your lives in imitation of him." This religious motivation of hagiography does not mean that the authors had no other goals in mind when they wrote their stories. Often they vigorously promote their particular church against other religious centers for ecclesiastical influence or to draw pilgrims to their shrines. But in spite of other motives, hagiography remains fundamentally a lesson in living the ideal Christian life.

Muirchú's *Life of Saint Patrick* follows the pattern found in most hagiography—origins, commissioning by God, miracles and wonders, death, and continued divine influence—but with the skill of a great storyteller and the passion to present his hero as the equal of other famous figures of the Christian faith. Muirchú draws on the gospels, the stories and prophets of the Hebrew Bible, and earlier saints' lives for his material, but he also had access to and uses at least a portion of the letters of Patrick himself.

The Latin text with translation and linguistic commentary is found in Ludwig Bieler, *The Patrician Texts in the Book of Armagh*, 62–123, 193–213.

A very helpful translation with notes is in Thomas O'Loughlin, *Discovering Saint Patrick*, 192–229. O'Loughlin's chapter on Muirchú in the same volume (112–130) is an excellent introduction to various aspects of the writer and his work.

There is much uncertainty and scholarly disagreement concerning the place names in Muirchú's text, so I have generally avoided trying to identify them in the notes. For possible locations of the places mentioned, see Bieler (referenced above) and Liam De Paor, *Saint Patrick's World*, 175–197.

❧

PROLOGUE

Many, my lord Áed,[1] have attempted to set down an account of this story according to what they heard from their fathers and from those who told it from the beginning.[2] But because of the great difficulties in telling this story and the differing opinions, and the numerous suspicions of many people, they were never able to agree on one, sure description of what happened.

So, if I may be frank, just as in the proverb of children being led forth into the amphitheater, I set out into the treacherous deep sea of telling a sacred story as if in a poor little boat in the midst of rocky reefs and swelling waves towering above me, off into uncharted waters,[3] traveled by none before me except my father Cogitosus.[4]

So that I don't seem to make something large out of a small thing, I will only tell a few of the many stories about holy Patrick. I do this with little prior experience, relying on uncertain sources, with my poor memory and feeble intellect, and in an unpolished style of writing. Still, I set forth in obedience to your command with the most pious affection of holy love because of your affection and authority.

> *In the name of the king of heaven, the savior of the universe.*
> *Here begins the prologue of the life of holy Patrick the confessor.*[5]

The time from the passion of our Lord Jesus Christ until the death of Patrick is 436 years.

I have discovered four names of Patrick in a book written by Ultán, bishop of Connor.[6] The first is Holy Magonus, meaning "famous." The second is Sochet....[7] The third is Patrick's own name, and the fourth is Cothirthiacus,[8] because he was a slave to four houses of druids. One of these druids named Míluch moccu Bóin bought him so that Patrick served in his house for seven years. Thus Patrick the son of Calfornius[9] had four names: Sochet when he was born, Cothirthiacus while he was a slave, Magonus as a student, and Patrick when he was ordained.

PATRICK'S CHILDHOOD AND CAPTIVITY

Patrick was known as Sochet and was born in Britain. His father was Calfornius, a deacon. Patrick tells us his father was the son of the priest Potitus who lived in Bannavem Thaburniae,[10] close to our sea. I am reliably told that this place is what is now called Ventre.[11] Patrick's mother was named Concessa.

When he was sixteen years old, he was along with others brought to this barbarian island and held as a slave by a cruel pagan king. He labored for him for six years, as in the Hebrew law,[12] with fear of God and trembling, as the psalmist says,[13] with vigils and many prayers. He prayed a hundred times each day and a hundred times by night, joyfully giving to God what were the things of God and to Caesar the things of Caesar.[14]

He began to fear and love the Lord almighty. Until that time he did not know the true God, but then his spirit began to burn inside him. After many hardships there, after hunger and thirst, after cold and nakedness, after laboring to care for sheep, after frequent visits from an angel named Victoricus,[15] after many famous miracles, after divine messages—I will mention only two examples: "You have fasted well, soon you will return to your country," and "Behold your ship is ready," which was not nearby but perhaps two hundred miles away in a place he had never been—after all these things, which hardly anyone could recount, when he was twenty-three he left his pagan master to his own life and with the sacred friendship of the eternal God of heaven he sailed in the ship prepared for him back to Britain with pagan barbarians who were worshipers of many false gods.

WANDERING THROUGH THE WILDERNESS

Like Jonah,[16] *after three days* and nights on the sea with these wicked men, Patrick traveled twenty-eight days through a deserted place, like Moses, though in a somewhat different way.

The pagans complained just as the Jews that they were almost dead from hunger and thirst.[17] The ship's captain taunted Patrick, asking him to call on his god to rescue them from death. Patrick was moved by their suffering and pitied the men. He was grieving in his spirit, but crowned with worthiness and glorified by God. And so Patrick, with God's help, supplied them with abundant food from a herd of pigs, just as God once sent a flock of quail to the Jews.[18] Like John the Baptist,[19] they also found wild honey. But as was proper for wicked pagans, they received pigs instead of locusts. But Patrick ate none of the food, for it had been offered in sacrifice.[20] Nonetheless he remained well, suffering neither hunger nor thirst.

On that same night while he slept, Satan attacked him fiercely. Patrick felt as if he had great rocks crushing his limbs. But twice he called on Elijah; then the sun rose on him, shining brightly and dispelling all the shadows of darkness and restoring his strength.

THE SECOND CAPTIVITY

Many years later he was once again captured by strangers. On the first night he was given a divine message saying to him: "You will be with them, your enemies, for two months." And so it was. After sixty days the Lord freed him from their hands, giving Patrick and his companions food, fire, and dry weather each day until the tenth day when they came upon other people.

HOME AGAIN

Again after a few years Patrick was back in his own land with his parents as in his youth. They welcomed him home as their son and begged him that after so many trials and tribulations he would not leave them again. But he did not agree. There he received many visions.

SETTING OUT FOR ROME

He was now approaching his thirtieth year and, as the apostle says, a mature man in the measure of the fullness of Christ.[21] He left home to visit and pay honor to the apostolic bishop,[22] the head of all the churches of the entire world. He desired to learn and understand and be filled with the divine wisdom and holy mysteries to which God was calling him, so that he might preach and bring divine grace to a distant people and convert them to faith in Christ.

BISHOP GERMANUS

Patrick crossed the sea south of Britain and began his journey across Gaul. He hoped to cross the Alps to journey to his final destination of Rome. On the way he discovered a very holy bishop of the city of Auxerre, the great Germanus,[23] who was a wonderful gift to him. Patrick remained with him a long time, just as Paul sat at the feet of Gamaliel.[24] There with great discipline, patience, and obedience he learned knowledge, wisdom, chastity, and everything useful for mind and soul as he had desired. With great fear and love of God, with goodness and simplicity of heart, a virgin in body and spirit, he learned, loved, and practiced the joy of his heart.

CALLED BACK TO IRELAND

After many years in Gaul—some say forty, others thirty—his faithful friend Victoricus, who had told him everything that would happen to him while a slave in Ireland, came to him in frequent visions and revealed to him that the time had come to fish with the net of the gospel among the untamed barbarians God had sent him among to teach. In a vision he told him, among other things, that "the sons and daughters of the wood of Foclut[25] call you."

Palladius

When the right moment had arrived, Patrick set out with God's help on the gospel journey for which he had long prepared himself. Germanus sent with him the priest Segitius so that he might have a companion as a witness, because Patrick had not yet been ordained as a bishop by the holy lord Germanus.

They knew for certain that Palladius, archdeacon of Pope Celestine,[26] the bishop of the city of Rome and forty-fifth in succession from holy Peter the apostle, had been ordained and sent to convert this island in the cold north. But Palladius was not successful because no one is able to receive anything unless it has been given to him by heaven.[27] This untamed and hostile people did not readily accept his teachings nor did he want to spend much time in a land that was not his own. So Palladius began his return journey to the one who had sent him. But on his way back from here, having crossed the first sea and started his travels on land, he died in the island of the Britons.

Consecrated as Bishop

In Ebmoria, Patrick heard of the death of holy Palladius in Britain from his returning disciples Augustine, Benedict, and others. He and his companions then traveled to meet a certain remarkable man and great bishop named Amathorex[28] who lived nearby. There holy Patrick, knowing what would happen to him,[29] accepted the rank of bishop from the holy bishop Amathorex. Auxilius, Iserninus, and the rest received lesser grades of ordination on the same day Patrick was consecrated.

When they had accepted the blessings according to custom, they sang the words of the psalmist especially appropriate for Patrick: "You are a priest in the eternal order of Melchizedek."[30] The experienced traveler then went on board a ship that was waiting and in the name of the holy Trinity crossed to Britain. He allowed no delays not required by the normal conditions of such a journey, for no one seeks the Lord with idleness. And so he crossed our sea quickly with a favorable wind.

King Loíguire

In those days there was in Ireland a certain fierce and mighty pagan king who ruled the barbarians and reigned at Tara, the capital of the land. His name was Loíguire son of Níall, the leader of the family that ruled almost all of this island.

He surrounded himself with wise men, druids, soothsayers, sorcerers, and every sort of man skilled in the craft of evil. By their pagan arts they were able to forecast and see ahead of time everything before it happened. The king preferred two of these men above all the rest—Lothroch, also called Lochru, and Lucet Máel, known as Ronal. This pair by their magic frequently foretold of a foreign way of life that would soon arrive, a kingdom from across the sea bringing unknown and dangerous teachings. Only a few would come bringing this doctrine, but it would be received by many. It would be honored by all and overthrow kingdoms. Kings who resisted it would be killed, the people would be seduced, all their gods would be destroyed, their skills and craft would be outlawed, and the new teaching would reign forever.

They told of the man who would bring this new teaching to the island and persuade the people. They prophesied concerning him in the following words with a poem that was often recited, especially in the two or three years before Patrick's arrival. These are the words of the poem. Because of the strange language it is hard to understand:

A man with a shaved head will come with a stick bent at the top.
He will sing evil songs from his house with a hole in its roof.
From a table at the front of his house
all his family will reply to him: "Let it be, let it be."[31]

In our own language we can say this more clearly: "When these things happen, our pagan kingdom will fall." This is of course what happened later when Patrick came and destroyed the worship of idols and the universal faith of Christ filled our land. But enough of these things. Let us return to our story.

PATRICK ARRIVES IN IRELAND

When his holy voyage was at an end, the ship of the holy man, heavy with wonders and treasures of the spirit from beyond the sea, arrived at a suitable harbor in the region of Cúala, a well-known port of our island called Inber Dee.

It seemed most fitting to him to redeem himself from slavery. Thus he was eager to journey north to the man named Miliucc who had held him in captivity. Patrick carried with him twice the earthly and heavenly ransom so that he might buy himself out of slavery from the man who had once owned him.

He turned his ship toward an island in the east that is now named for him, then leaving Brega and the lands of Conaille and the Ulaid on one side, he sailed to the inlet of Bréne. There he and those with him landed at Inber Sláne and hid their boat, then went a short distance inland to rest. A swineherd found them there. He was a servant of a man of natural goodness named Díchu, who lived in the place where a barn is now named for Patrick. The swineherd thought that they were thieves or robbers and ran to tell his master Díchu, then quietly led him to them. Díchu had in mind to kill them, but when he saw the face of holy Patrick, the Lord changed his thoughts to good. Patrick preached the faith to him and Díchu believed, being the first man to do so. Patrick stayed with him several days.

Patrick was eager to find Miliucc and buy his freedom as well as convert him to faith in Christ, so he left his ship with Díchu and set out across the lands of the Cruithni until he reached Slíab Míss.[32] This was the mountain where when he was held captive many years before he had seen the angel Victoricus leave his footprint swiftly on the rock of another mountain as he rose into the heavens in his sight.

The Death of Miliucc

When Miliucc heard that his slave was on his way to find him, he judged he did not want to change his ways by force at the end of his life so that the man who was once his slave might not rule over him. Prompted by the devil, Miliucc decided to end his own life with fire. He gathered together all his goods into the house where he had ruled as king and set it and himself ablaze.

Holy Patrick was standing on the right slope of Slíab Míss where he could see for the first time the land of his slavery and grace since his return. There is a cross there now to mark the spot. He gazed upon the fire of Miliucc with his own eyes. Patrick was so shocked by the sight that he stood there for two or three hours in silence, sighing and moaning and weeping the whole time.

Then he spoke: "I do not know, God knows. This man at the end of his days submitted himself to fire rather than serve the eternal God. I do not know, God knows. None of his sons will rule over his kingdom in the future. His descendants will serve others forevermore."

When he had said this he prayed and armed himself with the sign of the cross, then he turned and went back to the lands of the Ulaid the same way he had come. He traveled to Mag Inis and Díchu, staying there several days going around the whole plain. He chose the area as a place he loved. It was there the faith began to grow.

The Angel

Now let us return to the earlier story. An angel used to visit him on the seventh day of each week. Patrick enjoyed conversing with the angel as one man speaks with another. When he was captured at sixteen and endured six years of slavery, the angel came and spoke with him thirty times. Patrick enjoyed his conversations and advice before he journeyed from Ireland to the land of the Romans. Once he lost a herd of pigs when he was watching over them, but the angel came and showed him where they were. Another day after Patrick and the angel had been speaking about many things, the angel put his foot on the Rock of Scirit next to Slíab Miss and ascended in his presence. The footprint can still be seen and is the place where the angel spoke to him thirty times. It is now a place of prayer where the supplications of the faithful produce happy fruit.

Preparing for Easter

Now in those days Easter was drawing near. This was the first Easter celebrated in the Egypt which is this island as in the land of Goshen.[33] Patrick and his companions talked about where they might celebrate this first Easter among the gentiles to which God had sent them. After discussing many possibilities, at last holy Patrick was inspired by God and decided that this solemn festival of the Lord, the greatest of all festivals, should be celebrated in the wide plain of Brega. In that place was the mightiest kingdom of all the Irish tribes, the center of their paganism and idolatry. There he would, as the psalm says, crush the head of the dragon[34] and drive an unbreakable wedge into the head of all idolatry so that no other faith might rise against Christ. This would be done for the first time by the spiritual hands of holy Patrick and his companions with the hammer of brave deeds along with faith. And so it was done.

The Easter Celebration

They set out on the sea in their ship from Mag Inis and bade farewell to the good man Díchu who was full of peace and faith. To carry out in full their ministry they sailed with the coast on their right hand, as is proper, as it was on their left side before.

After an easy and calm trip they arrived at Inber Colpdi and left behind their boat there. Then they traveled by foot to the great plain. As evening fell they finally arrived at the burial mounds of the men of Fíacc. Ferchertne, one of the nine wise prophets of

Brega, says they were built by the man-servants of Fíacc. There Patrick and his companions set up camp and offered, as the prophet says, a fitting Easter sacrifice of praise to the most high God with full devotion of spirit.

The Pagan Feast at Tara

At the same time that year the heathens were celebrating a pagan ceremony with many incantations, magical rites, and idolatrous superstitions. Kings were there with satraps, leaders, princes, and all the nobility, along with druids, fortunetellers, and all those skilled in the dark arts. Loíguire summoned them all to Tara just as King Nebuchadnezzar once called such men to Babylon.[35] They held their heathen celebration on the same night that holy Patrick was celebrating Easter.

There was a tradition among them made known to all that if anyone near or far kindled a fire on that night before the king had lit his in his palace at Tara, that man would forfeit his life. But holy Patrick lit his bright and blessed sacred Easter fire that night and it was seen by all those who lived in the plain. Everyone at Tara who saw the fire stared at it with amazement.

The king called together all his elders and demanded from them: "Who has dared to commit such a crime in my kingdom? Let him be killed!" They all replied that they did not know who lit the fire. But then the druids said, "King, may you live forever![36] This fire we see lit on this night before your own, unless it is extinguished tonight it will never die and it will outshine all the fires of our own ways. The one who kindled it and the kingdom he brings this night will overcome you and all of us, seducing the people of your realm. All our kingdoms will fall before it as it fills the whole land and rules forever.

The Easter Fire

As it was in the days of Herod,[37] when King Loíguire heard these things he was greatly troubled and all of Tara with him. He answered and said: "This shall not be! Now we will go up and see what has happened. We will capture and slay those who do these evil deeds in our kingdom."

The king ordered three times nine chariots made ready, according to the tradition of their gods, and took with him Lucet Máel and Lochru, his two most powerful druids in contests of power. They left Tara at the end of the night and went toward the burial ground of the men of Fíacc, with the faces of men and horses turned to the left as was fitting.

As they traveled, the druids said to Loíguire: "O King, do not go to the place where the fire is yourself. If you do, you might afterward submit to the man who lit it. Instead, stay outside and order that man to go to you so that he might submit to you and you rule over him. Then we will debate with that man before you, O king, and you may judge between us." The king answered them and said: "This is good advice. I will do as you have said." Then they came to the place and dismounted from their horses and chariots, but they did not enter the circle of light. Instead they sat down outside of it.

Patrick and the King

Thus the king summoned holy Patrick outside the light of the fire. The druids said to themselves, "Let us not stand up when he comes here, for whoever rises at his coming will afterward believe in him and obey him."

When Patrick came to them and saw the great number of their chariots and horses, the fitting verse of the psalmist was on his lips and in his heart: "Some come in chariots and some on horses, but we will walk in the name of our God."[38] They did not rise up at his approach, except for one who was prompted by the Lord to disobey the command of the druids. This was Ercc, son of Daig, whose relics are now adored in the town called Slane. He stood and Patrick blessed him, and he believed in the everlasting God.

The debate then began with the druid called Lochru taunting holy Patrick and mocking the universal faith with wicked words. As he said such things, holy Patrick looked him in the eye and—just as Peter had once done with Simon—spoke to the Lord confidently with powerful words: "Lord, you who hold power over everything and whose power holds together all things, it is you who sent me here. Raise up this impious man who blasphemes your name. Cast him out and let him die a sudden death." At these words the druid was lifted up into the air and fell down again, splitting open his skull on a rock. He died in front of everyone, and the pagans were afraid.

The Punishment of God

The king and his men were so angry with Patrick that they wanted to kill him. The king ordered: "Seize this man who is destroying us!" When holy Patrick saw that the wicked pagans were about to attack him, he shouted: "Let God rise up, let his enemies be scattered, and let those who hate him flee from his face."[39] Immediately darkness fell and a horrible tumult arose as the wicked men fought among themselves. A great earthquake struck and the axles of their chariots smashed against each other. Their horses and chariots were driven violently through the plain until only a few of the men escaped half-alive to Mount Monduirn. Seven times seven men perished before the very eyes of the king because of his own words. The four who alone remained alive were the king, his wife, and two other Irishmen, but these four were very afraid.

The queen approached Patrick and said to him: "O just and powerful man, do not destroy the king. He is coming to you on bended knee to worship your lord."

The king, compelled by fear, then came forward and fell on his knees before the holy man to honor him, but he did not wish to. After he had gone a little way from Patrick, the king called the holy man to him and pretended to be kind, though in fact he wished to kill him.

Patrick, however, knew what the wicked king planned to do. Patrick blessed his own companions, eight men and a boy, in the name of Jesus Christ, then they started to walk toward the king. Loíguire counted them as they approached, but suddenly they disappeared from before his eyes. All he saw were eight deer and a fawn going as if into the wilderness. Loíguire was then sorrowful, afraid, and greatly shamed as he returned to Tara at dawn with those few who had escaped.

Patrick at Tara

Easter was the next day and the kings, princes, and druids were all feasting with King Loíguire, for this was the day of their greatest festival. They were eating and drinking wine in the palace at Tara. Some were talking and others were thinking about the things that had happened. Suddenly holy Patrick and five of his companions entered through closed doors—just as it is said Christ did[40]—so that he could preach and show forth the sacred faith at Tara before all the people.

When he entered the feasting hall of Tara, no one rose up to welcome him except a single man, Dubthach maccu Lugir, who was the greatest poet. There was a young man with him named Fíacc who was then still a boy, though afterward he became a famous bishop whose relics are adored at Sléibte. Dubthach, as I have said, was the only one of the pagans to rise in honor of holy Patrick. The holy man blessed him and on that day he was the first to believe in God, and it was counted unto him as righteousness.[41]

When the pagans saw Patrick, they asked him to eat with them so that they might test him. Patrick, knowing what was about to happen,[42] did not refuse their invitation.

THE MIRACLES OF PATRICK

While everyone was eating, one of the druids named Lucet Máel was eager on that day to challenge holy Patrick. This man had taken part in the conflict with Patrick the previous night in which his fellow druid had been killed. Lucet Máel put a drop of poison from his cup into the cup of Patrick while everyone was watching to see what would happen. When Patrick saw he was being tested, he blessed his cup as everyone looked on so that the liquid in the cup froze like ice. He then turned the cup upside down, but then only the drop the magician had added fell out. Patrick then blessed the cup again and the liquid in the cup melted again while all watched in amazement.

After a short time the druid said: "Let us perform wonders on this wide plain."[43] And Patrick said, "What kind of wonders should we perform?" And the druid said, "Let us call down snow to cover the land." But Patrick said, "I do not want to do anything contrary to the will of God." And the druid said, "I will call down snow for all to see." He then uttered magical spells and called down snow so that it fell over the whole plain up to the depth of a man's belt, while everyone was amazed.

Then holy Patrick said: "We have seen what you can do. Now remove the snow." The druid said: "I cannot remove it until this same time tomorrow." And the holy man said: "You can work evil, but not good. This is not so for me." He then blessed the whole field. Without rain, mist, or wind, the snow disappeared immediately. The crowd was amazed and cheered and their hearts were touched.

A little while later, the druid invoked demons and called down darkness on the whole land as a marvel. The people were angry and muttered against him. Holy Patrick then said, "Remove the darkness." But again the druid was not able to do it. But the holy man said a prayer and drove away the darkness. The sun shined forth and everyone shouted with thanks and gladness.

After these contests between the druid and Patrick in the presence of the king, Loíguire said to them, "Throw your books into the water. I will honor the man whose books are not damaged." And Patrick responded, "I will do as you ask." But the druid said: "I do not want to be judged by means of water with this man, for water is a god to him." He had heard that Patrick baptized with water.

The king therefore said, "Then use fire." And Patrick said, "I am ready to do this." But the druid refused him, saying "This man worships fire and water in alternate years." And the holy man said, "That is not true. You and one of my boys go into an enclosed house which is divided in two parts. You wear my robe while my boy wears yours. Both of you then shall be set on fire and judged in the sight of the Most High."

They all agreed on this and built a house constructed with half green wood and half dry wood. The druid went into the part with the green wood while one of holy Patrick's boys named Benignus went into the part made of dry wood wearing the robe of the druid. The building was then closed up and set on fire while the whole crowd watched.

And so it happened in that hour that through the prayers of Patrick the flames consumed the druid and the green wood of the house completely. Only Patrick's robe survived untouched by the fire. The opposite happened to happy Benignus. Although he was in the part of the structure made with dry wood, it was as it is written of the three young men, that the fire did not touch him at all and gave him no pain or distress. Only the druid's robe which he wore was burned, according to the will of God.

The king was very angry with Patrick because of the death of the druid and would have killed him, but God prevented him. But by the prayer of Patrick and by his word the anger of God fell upon those wicked people so that many of them perished. Holy Patrick then said to the king, "Unless you now believe, you will die, for the anger of God has come upon your head." And the king was very afraid. His heart was greatly troubled and all of Tara with him.

The Conversion of Loíguire

At last King Loíguire called all his elders and his advisors to him and said, "It is better for me to believe than die." After this meeting he consented to the advice of his councilors and on that day converted to the eternal Lord God, while many others believed as well. Holy Patrick then said to him, "You resisted my teachings and were an impediment to me, therefore the days of your own reign shall continue, but none of your descendants will be king after you."

Following the teachings of the Lord Jesus, holy Patrick left there and went forth to teach all people, baptizing them in the name of the Father and of the Son and of the Holy Spirit.[44] He preached everywhere with the Lord helping him by confirming his words with miracles.

The Wondrous Deeds of Patrick

With the help of God, I will now try to relate just a few of the many wonders done by Patrick. He was, if I may say so, the bishop and teacher of all of Ireland.

Monesan the Virgin

During the time when all of Britain was frozen in unbelief, there was a certain remarkable daughter of a king by the name of Monesan. She was filled with the Holy Spirit, who helped her not to yield to the many men who sought to marry her. Even though she was frequently drenched with water, she would not consent to what she believed was wrong and a less worthy life.

In between the beatings and drenching to persuade her to marry, she kept asking her mother and nurse who had made the spheres of heaven that gave light to the world. When she was told that the one who made the sun had his seat in heaven, she, though repeatedly urged to submit to the bonds of marriage, was inspired by the Holy Spirit to say: "Never will I do this." For she was seeking through nature the creator of all creation just as Abraham had done.

Her sorrowful parents were considering what to do with her when they heard of Patrick, a just man, who was visited by the eternal God every seventh day. They then took their daughter to Ireland to look for Patrick and with great effort found him. He asked them why they had come and they said, "The burning desire of our daughter to see God has forced us to come to you." Then Patrick was filled with the Holy Spirit, lifted up his voice and said to the young woman, "Do you believe in God?" And she replied, "I do." Then he baptized her with water and the Holy Spirit.

Immediately she fell down dead on the ground and gave her spirit into the hands of the angels. She was buried where she had died. Patrick then prophesied that after twenty years her body would be carried with honor from that place to a nearby chapel, and so it was done. The relics of the young woman from across the sea are adored there to this day.

The Wicked British King

I cannot pass over in silence another of Patrick's amazing deeds. He had heard the news of the wicked actions of a certain British king named Corotic, a cruel and horrible tyrant, who was a great persecutor and murderer of Christians.[45] Patrick had written him a letter trying to call him back to the way of truth, but Corotic only laughed at his warnings. When Patrick was told of this, he prayed to the Lord and said, "Lord, if it is possible, expel this faithless man from your presence now and forever more."

One day not long after this, Corotic heard music and someone singing that he should leave his throne. Then all those dearest to him burst into this same song. Corotic, suddenly in the middle of his hall, was shamefully changed into a fox and ran away. Since that time, he has not been seen again, like water that has flowed away.

The Boy Benignus

I should briefly mention another miracle accomplished by the godly and apostolic man Patrick while he was still in the flesh. This deed is recorded as being done only by Patrick and Stephen.

Once when Patrick was going to his accustomed place to pray alone at night, he saw the wonders of heaven. Wishing to test his beloved and faithful holy boy, he said to him, "My son, please tell me if you see what I see." Then the boy named Benignus immediately said to him, "I know what you sense, for I see heaven open and the son of God and his angels."[46] Then Patrick said, "Now I know that you are worthy to be my successor."

They continued walking and soon came to Patrick's usual place of prayer. While they were praying there in the middle of a stream, the boy said, "I cannot bear this cold water." For the water was very cold. Then Patrick told him to go from the upper part of the stream to the lower part. There he admitted that he was also unable to remain long since the water was too warm. Not able to stay there, he climbed out of the stream onto dry land.

Macc Cuill moccu Graccae

In the days of Patrick there lived a man in the lands of the Ulaid named Macc Cuill moccu Graccae. He was a wicked and savage tyrant, so much so that he was called the Cyclops. His thoughts were depraved, his words intemperate, his deeds wicked, his spirit bitter, his temper full of anger, his body full of sin, his mind cruel, his life pagan, and his conscience most foolish.

This man had sunk so low in wickedness that one day while he was sitting on a wild, towering hill in Druim moccu Echach—a place where he daily carried out his tyranny, wearing the signs of his harsh cruelty, and murdering travelers as they passed by—he saw holy Patrick coming near, shining as if with the bright light of faith and the crown of heavenly glory, making his way with the untroubled trust that came from his teaching. The outlaw then said to his wicked companions, "Look, there is the man who seduces the people and leads them astray. He carries out his tricks to deceive people. Let's go and test him so that we can find out if this god he glorifies has any power."

So they tested the holy man by putting one of their number who was in perfectly good health in the middle of them under a cloak and pretended he was terribly ill. They did this to prove the holy man was a fraud and to show he misled people, to reveal his miracles as mere tricks, and to show his prayers were evil incantations.

When Patrick and his disciples approached, the pagans said to him, "Look, one of our companions is sick. Come and sing some of the incantations of your religion over him so that he might be healed." Holy Patrick knew their evil deeds and tricks, so he firmly said to them without fear, "If he had truly been sick his present condition would be no surprise to you." They then uncovered the face of their companion who had pretended he was sick and saw that he was now dead.

The pagans were astonished by such a wonder and spoke among themselves: "Truly, this is a man of God. It was sinful of us to put him to a test." Holy Patrick then turned to Macc Cuill and said, "Why did you want to test me?" The cruel tyrant then said, "I am sorry I did this to you. Whatever you ask of me, I will do. I now submit myself to the power of the great God whose way you preach." The holy man then said, "Believe therefore in my God the Lord Jesus and be baptized in the name of the Father and Son and Holy Spirit." Macc Cuill turned that hour to the eternal God and was baptized.

Then Macc Cuill continued, "I confess to you, my holy master Patrick, that I had planned to murder you. Judge therefore what price I must pay for such a great crime." And Patrick said, "I am not able to judge you, but God will. Therefore go down to the seashore unarmed and immediately leave this region of Ireland. Take nothing with you from your goods except a worn garment that barely covers your body. Do not eat or drink anything of the fruit of this island since you have the mark of your sins upon your head. When you come to the sea, lock your feet in iron chains and throw the key into the waves. Then push off to sea in a boat only one skin thick without rudder or oar. Be prepared to go wherever the winds and sea will take you. Wherever God's providence sends you, there live and obey his divine commands." And Macc Cuill answered, "I will do as you have said. But what should we do about this dead man?" And Patrick said, "He will live and rise without pain." In that same hour Patrick raised him from the dead and returned him to health.

Then Macc Cuill left with the confidence of certain faith and went to the shore south of Mag Inis. He fettered his feet and threw the key into the sea as he had been told. Then he climbed into the little boat and set out.

The north wind blew him southward until he came to an island called Euonia.[47] There he found two excellent men splendid in faith and teaching. They had been the first to teach the word of God in Euonia and by their teaching had converted the people of the island to the universal faith. Their names were Conindrus and Rumilus. These two were amazed when they saw the man dressed in his single garment and had pity on him. They led him from the sea and embraced him with joy. Thus he found spiritual fathers in a place appointed to him by God and trained his body and spirit to obey their instruction. He spent the rest of his life on that island with these two holy bishops until he became their successor. This is Macc Cuill, bishop of Mane and prelate of Arde Huimnonn.

The Pagans Working on Sunday

At another time holy Patrick was resting on a Sunday beside a marsh on the seashore not far north of Druimm Bó. While he was there he heard the loud noise of some pagans digging a ditch around a fort. He called to them and ordered them not to work on the Lord's day, but they ignored the words of the holy man and laughed at him. Then holy Patrick said, "Mudebroth![48] You will gain nothing from all your work." And that was what happened. The next night a great wind rose up and stirred the waves destroying all the work of the pagans, just as the holy man said.

Dáire and His Horse

Once there was a wealthy and honored man in the eastern lands by the name of Dáire. Patrick asked him if he would grant him some land to practice his religion. The rich man said to the holy man, "What land do you want?" The holy man said, "I would like that high piece of land that is called Druimm Sailech so that I may build on it." But Dáire did not want to give the holy man that high ground, so he gave him a piece of low ground where there is now the burial ground of martyrs near Armagh. Holy Patrick settled there with his followers.

One day a man who looked after Dáire's horses brought one of the animals to let it graze in the meadow of the Christians. Patrick was offended by the release of the horse on his piece of land and said to the servant, "Dáire has been foolish to send a brute animal to disturb a place he gave to God." But the servant said nothing as if he were deaf and a mute who does not open his mouth. He went away and left the horse in the field for the night.

The next day the servant came to bring the horse back but found it dead. He returned sadly to his master's house and said to him, "That Christian killed your horse because it offended him to have that placed disturbed." Dáire said to his men, "That man must die. Go now and kill him."

But just as the men were going out, Dáire fell down dead. His wife then said, "The Christian is the cause of his death. Someone go quickly to seek his blessing and you will be well. Call back also those who went to kill the Christian." Two men then went out and spoke to Patrick, hiding what had happened, "Dáire is sick. Give us something to bring to him so that he might be well." But holy Patrick, knowing all that had happened, said to them, "Is that so?" Then he blessed some water and gave it to them saying, "Go sprinkle this on your horse, then take the animal with you." They did so and the horse came back to life. When they sprinkled the water on Dáire he was revived as well.

Dáire then came to honor holy Patrick and brought as a gift a wonderful bronze cauldron from overseas which held three measures. Dáire said to the holy man, "Behold, this bronze cauldron is yours." And holy Patrick said, "Thank you." Dáire went home and said to his household, "This man is a fool. I gave him a wonderful bronze cauldron that holds three measures and all he says is 'Thank you'."[49] Dáire then said to his servants, "Go bring my cauldron back." They went out and said to Patrick, "We are taking back the cauldron." Patrick then said, "Thank you. Take it away." And so they did. Dáire then asked his men, "What did the Christian say when you took back the cauldron?" They answered, "He said, 'Thank you'." Dáire then said, "'Thank you' for giving and 'Thank you' for taking. This is such a good response that because of his 'Thank you' I will give him the cauldron back again."

Dáire himself went to Patrick straightaway with the cauldron and said to him, "This cauldron is yours to keep since you are a steady man who is not easily disturbed. Moreover I now grant to you that piece of land you first requested so that you may live there." That is the city now called Armagh.

Patrick and Dáire then went out to inspect the generous and pleasing gift. On the top of the hill they found a doe with her small fawn lying in the place where now is the altar of the northern church at Armagh. The companions of Patrick wanted to capture and kill the fawn, but the holy man told them not to. He took up the fawn and carried it on his shoulders while the doe followed him meekly like a loving lamb to a nearby meadow north of Armagh. There, as wise men tell us, the signs of his wondrous powers continue to this day.

The Curse of Patrick

Reliable sources say that there was once a very harsh and greedy man living in Mag Inis. One day when two oxen which drew the cart of Patrick were resting and grazing in his meadow after their holy work, that foolish man angrily drove them away within the presence of holy Patrick. He grew angry and cursed that man saying, "*Mude-broth!* You have sinned. This field will never again profit either you or your descendants. From now on it will be useless to you."

And so it was. That same day a flood from the sea came and washed over the whole field. And so a fruitful land became a marsh because of the sins of those dwelling there, as the prophet says. It has been sandy and barren from the day when holy Patrick cursed it to this present day.

THE PRAYERS OF PATRICK

I will record a few of the many things I might say concerning the diligence of Patrick's prayers. Whether he was in one place or traveling, each day Patrick would sing psalms, hymns, the Apocalypse of John, and all the spiritual songs of the scriptures. Each hour of the day and night he would make the sign of the cross upon himself a hundred times. And whenever he saw a cross he would come down from his chariot and go before it to pray.

A Dead Man Speaks

One day when Patrick was on a journey, he passed by a cross on the side of the road that he didn't see, but his charioteer did. When they came to a guest house that had been their destination, they prayed before eating. Then the driver said, "I saw a cross that we passed on the side of the road."

Patrick left the guest house and went back along the road they had taken, praying as he went until he saw the grave. He asked the dead man buried there how he had died and whether he had been a Christian. The dead man said, "I was a pagan when I was buried here. But there was a woman from another province whose son had died here far away from her. She wasn't here when he was buried, but later she came here to mourn and lament her lost son. She was so upset that she mistook my pagan grave for his, thinking it belonged to her son and so she placed a cross here."

Patrick said that he had not seen the cross since it was the grave of a pagan. But Patrick's great power is made manifest in this story because he caused a dead man to speak. The man who had died in the faith was then honored and the nourishing cross was moved to its rightful place next to his grave.

The Lost Horses

It was Patrick's custom not to travel from the evening of the Lord's night[50] until the morning of the second day of the week. One Sunday when he was spending the night in a field at this sacred time, a great rain storm began. Although the whole land was drenched with heavy rain, the spot where the holy bishop stayed remained dry, as in the story of Gideon's bowl and fleece.[51]

Then Patrick's charioteer realized the horses had wandered away and wept for them as for dear friends since he was unable to search for them because of the darkness. This stirred the compassion of father Patrick and he said to the weeping charioteer, "God always hears us in our great sorrows and will help us now. You will find the horses you are weeping about."

Then Patrick rolled up his sleeve, drew out his hand, and raised his five fingers in the air so that they shone forth over the land with light. The charioteer then found his lost horses and stopped weeping, but he did not make this miracle known until after Patrick's death.

Patrick's Four Petitions

After he had done so many miracles that the world now celebrates, some recorded and others passed on piously by word of mouth, the day of Patrick's death was approaching. An angel came to speak with him about it. Thus Patrick sent word to Armagh, because he loved that place above all the lands on earth. He ordered that many men should come and accompany him to the place he much desired. With his companions he then began the journey to his beloved Armagh, the land of his longing.

Next to the road there was a bush that burned but was not consumed, just as it was with Moses.[52] The angel Victor[53] who used to visit Patrick often was in the bush. Victor sent another angel to stop Patrick from going where he wished to go. This angel said to him, "Why do you go on a journey without consulting Victor? He is calling you now. Turn aside to see him." Patrick turned aside as he was commanded and asked Victor what he should do. The angel said, "Return to the place from which you came (i.e., to Saul) and the four petitions that you sought will be granted to you."

"The first petition is that your authority would be in Armagh. The second is that whoever sings the hymn composed about you on the day of his death will have his penance for sins decided by you. The third is that the descendants of Díchu, the man who welcomed you so kindly, will deserve mercy and not perish. The fourth petition is that all the Irish will be judged by you on the day of judgment—just as it was said to the apostles: 'And you shall sit judging the twelve tribes of Israel'[54]—so that you as their apostle might judge them. Go back therefore as I have told you, and when you die you will enter the way of your fathers."

And so it happened on the seventeenth of March—with the years of his life numbered one hundred and twenty[55]—and all of Ireland celebrates this day every year.

THE DEATH OF PATRICK

"And you will set a barrier against the night."[56]

On the day of Patrick's death and for twelve days afterward there was no night throughout the province while they celebrated his passing. Night did not rush down or embrace the earth with its dark wings. There was neither the dark of night nor did evening bring in the shadows bearing stars. The Ulaid say that until the end of the year in which he died the nights were not as dark as they had been before. Surely this was to declare the glories of such a great man.

If there is anyone who doubts that night was suspended and that darkness was not seen throughout the whole province during

the time Patrick was mourned, let him hear and pay careful attention to the story of Hezekiah.[57] As a sign of his healing, Hezekiah
saw the sun going backward over ten lines of the sundial of Ahaz
so that the day almost doubled in length. Remember also how the
sun stood still at Gibeon and the moon in the valley of Aijalon.[58]

When the hour of his death was approaching, Patrick had received the sacrament from bishop Tassach as food for his journey
to the blessed life, just as the angel Victor had told him.

The Vigil of Angels

Angels kept vigil over his beloved body with prayers and psalms
during the night after his death, for all the men who had come to
keep the vigil fell asleep. But during the other nights the men
prayed and sang psalms while they watched over the body. After
the angels had returned to heaven they left behind a very sweet
smell like honey or the sweet fragrance that comes from wine.
This fulfilled the blessing of the patriarch Jacob who said, "Behold,
the smell of my son is like a fruitful field blessed by the Lord."[59]

The Angel's Advice

An angel once came to Patrick and gave him advice about his
tomb.

"Choose two unbroken oxen and let them wander wherever
they will. Where they halt, build a church there in honor of your
remains." And as the angel said, the untamed oxen were chosen

and with a harness around their necks they pulled the cart carrying the holy body of Patrick. The place called Clocher to the east of Findabair was the place honored by the oxen of Conal. By the will of God they went to Dún Lethglaisse, where Patrick is buried.

The angel had said to Patrick, "So that your body will not be removed from the ground, let it be covered by a cubit of earth." The proof that this order came from God is shown by a recent event. When a church was being built there over the body, the men who were digging saw fire shoot up from Patrick's tomb and immediately they fled in terror of the flame.

The Contest for Patrick's Body

When holy Patrick died, a struggle over his relics arose that was so great it led to war between the Uí Néill and their eastern allies against the Ulaid. Once they were friendly neighbors, but now they are the most bitter of enemies. To prevent bloodshed, the inlet of the sea called Druimm Bó arose by the merits of Patrick and the mercy of God. It rose up high in swirling waves with their crests bursting through the air as in a race to quench the rage of these warring tribes, for that is the sort of people they are. Thus the rising of the sea stopped these tribes from fighting.

But after Patrick was buried and the sea had calmed, the easterners and the Uí Néill again rushed to battle with the Ulaid. Armed and prepared for war they invaded the resting place of his holy body, though they were thankfully misled by an illusion: They thought they saw two oxen pulling a cart and believed they were

seizing the holy body. With the body and all their weapons they
came as far as the Cabcenne River, but then the body vanished
from their sight. For it was not possible for there to be peace concerning such a famous and blessed body unless God gave them
such a vision at that time. The salvation of countless souls would
have been turned to destruction and death otherwise. In the same
way in ancient days, the Syrians were blinded so that they could
not kill the prophet Elisha.[60] By the providence of God they were
led by Elisha as far as Samaria. And in the way this illusion brought
peace to the people.

THE LIFE OF SAINT BRIGID

Unlike Patrick, there is little we can say with certainty about the life of the greatest female figure in Irish Christianity. The Irish annals say that Brigid was born in the middle of the fifth century and died about seventy years later, though the annals are not particularly reliable for early times. Brigid's service to God centered on the founding of a monastery primarily for women at Kildare (Irish *Cill Dara,* "the church of oak") on the fertile plains of Leinster west of modern Dublin. It was here that Brigid lived her life and carried out her tireless labor in a world dominated by men.

The miracles of Brigid recorded by Cogitosus are patterned largely on the life of Christ as recorded in the gospels. She provides food for the needy, turns water into beer, sides with the oppressed, and heals the sick. But unlike Jesus, she tames wild animals to her service and prompts domestic animals to act against their own instincts when needed. She bends the laws of nature to her will by transporting a large tree and moving a river, but most famously by hanging her cloak on a sunbeam. In a striking episode that has troubled some readers, she terminates the pregnancy of a young nun who has strayed from the path of chastity by placing her hands on the woman's womb and blessing her. Aside from one incident in which cattle thieves are drowned, she does not engage in the kind of dramatic and sometimes lethal battles against unbelievers attributed to Patrick. Brigid's miracles possess a sympathy of spirit, an unerring kindness, and a quality of gentleness lacking in the hagiography of many male saints.

It is no surprise that many scholars who have written about the Christian Brigid see in her life and cult aspects of pre-Christian Irish religion. It would have been natural for early Irish Christians to adopt certain aspects of earlier religion into their worship to attract converts, as was done elsewhere. It can scarcely be a coincidence that the feast day of Saint Brigid has from earliest times been February 1, the date of the important pre-Christian festival of Imbolc at the coming of spring and the start of the Irish agricultural season, heralded by the birth of lambs. Another possible connection to an earlier age is a story told by the visiting twelfth-century Welsh churchman Gerald. He describes an eternal fire kept burning at the church of Kildare which was tended only by nuns of Brigid's order. Any man who tried to cross the hedge surrounding the fire hut would supposedly be struck by madness or death.

But we must be cautious in proclaiming the Christian Brigid a baptized Celtic deity. The evidence of Gerald of Wales, for example, is problematic. Perpetual fires were also known in at least six other churches in early Ireland, all of them male monasteries. It is also troubling that Gerald's description of a cultic fire does not occur in any of the early lives of Brigid, including that of Cogitosus.

We know almost nothing about Cogitosus, the author of the *Life of Saint Brigid*. Muirchú, the author of the earliest life of Patrick, calls Cogitosus his father, but this is likely meant in a spiritual rather than biological sense. We know that Muirchú lived in the latter years of the seventh century, so assuming that his Cogitosus is the same as the writer of the *Life of Saint Brigid*, we can place our author in the mid-seventh century, more than a century after the reported death of Brigid. Although we know little about Cogitosus the man, we can say something about his style and goals. His Latin is good, indicating a solid monastic education. He is a strong advocate of the church at Kildare and was almost certainly a member of the monastic community there. In his introduction, Cogitosus assures his fellow clergymen that he has drawn on stories handed down by elders for his *Life*. After a standard protest that he is inadequate for the task at hand, he launches into his subject with enthusiasm. He states that his goal is to make better known the miraculous deeds of Brigid and claims that the monastery at Kildare exerts ecclesiastical supremacy over the whole land of Ireland from sea to sea—surely a deliberate challenge to the churchmen at Armagh in the north of the island who saw themselves as the leading Irish church.

Brigid's death, perhaps in the 520s, marked only the beginning of her influence in Ireland and beyond. Kildare grew in importance as an ecclesiastical center until it rivaled Armagh. Cogitosus asserts Kildare's claim to religious dominance over all of Ireland, but Brigid's monastery eventually recognized Armagh as the spiritual center of the island.

Even with the primacy of Armagh acknowledged, the influence of Brigid continued to grow. Several lives of Brigid were composed in Ireland in both Latin and Irish over the following centuries. The cult of Brigid spread to Britain and the continent with the travels of Irish missionaries and was embraced by Christians throughout Europe. In Ireland her renown continued to grow so that she became known as "Mary of the Irish" and her adoration was second only to Patrick. Wells dedicated to Brigid are found throughout the island, as are towns and churches named after her. Even today she is a subject of devotion among the faithful, especially women.

There is no modern edition of the Latin text of the *Life of Saint Brigid*. In my translation I have instead drawn on copies of several medieval manuscripts kindly provided to me by librarians in England, Belgium, Italy, Germany, and France.

Sean Connolly and J.-M. Picard have translated the entire text in the "Cogitosus's *Life of St. Brigit*" (117, 1987, 5–27).

The best books on Brigid and women in early Irish Christianity are Christina Harrington, *Women in a Celtic Church: Ireland 450–1150,* and Lisa Bitel, *Landscape with Two Saints*.

Two fundamental resources for early Irish culture are *A Guide to Early Irish Law* and *Early Irish Farming,* both by Fergus Kelly.

�֍

PROLOGUE

My brothers, you have compelled me to attempt to record, as if I were a learned man, the miracles and works of the virgin Brigid of holy and blessed memory, drawing on written documents and memories about her.[1] This task you impose on me is difficult because of its delicate subject matter and because I am unimportant, woefully ignorant, and have no talent for writing. But God is powerful enough to make great things from little, just as he did when he filled the house of the poor widow from a little jug of oil and a handful of grain.[2]

Since I must do as you have commanded, I am content that I have done my duty. I have resolved to make known a few of the many stories handed down by elders and those far more informed than I am. I present these plainly and without ambiguity to avoid the charge of disobedience.

Through these stories I hope that everyone will see the greatness and worth of the virgin abounding in glorious virtues. Not that my poor memory, my rustic style, or my lack of talent could ever be adequate to accomplish such a great duty. But your blessed faith and daily prayers can help me accomplish a task beyond the abilities of this poor narrator.

Brigid grew in extraordinary virtues so that news of her good works drew to her countless men and women from all the provinces of Ireland who freely made their vows to her. She built her own monastery in the broad plain of the Liffe on the firm foundation of faith. It is the head of almost all the churches of

Ireland and the surpassing leader of all the Irish monasteries. Its jurisdiction extends through the whole of Ireland from sea to sea.

Brigid worked diligently to see that all the souls in her care lived an orderly life and was greatly concerned for her followers in churches in all the provinces of the island. But she realized that she could not manage without a high priest who could consecrate churches and confer holy orders among them. She therefore sent for a renowned hermit known for his good qualities through whom God had worked many miracles. She called him from his hermitage and solitary life, setting out to meet him, so that he might govern with her as bishop and that nothing would be lacking regarding priestly offices in her churches.

And thus afterward the anointed head and leader of all the bishops along with the most blessed chief abbess of women ruled together over her first church in happy partnership guided by virtue. By the merits of both, their episcopal and feminine authority spread throughout the whole island of Ireland like a fruitful vine with growing branches. Her church has continued to be ruled in happy succession by the leader of the Irish bishops and the abbess whom all the abbesses of the Irish revere.

Thus, as I said above, since I have been compelled by my brothers, I will try to relate briefly and concisely the wonders performed by blessed Brigid, both those miracles done after she became an abbess and those done earlier, with the latter first.

THE LIFE OF SAINT BRIGID

The Family of Brigid

Holy Brigid was known to God before her birth and predestined to conform to his own image.[3] She was born in Ireland of noble Christian parents and came from the good and most wise tribe of Echtech. The name of her father was Dubthach and her mother Broicsech.[4] From her childhood she grew in her desire to do good. This girl chosen by God was full of self-restraint and modesty, always ripening into a better life.

But who could possibly tell of all her many works and wondrous deeds, even during the years of her youth? I will only relate a few of the countless miracles she performed as examples.

Butter for the Poor and Needy

When Brigid was old enough, one day her mother set her to the task of churning milk so that she could turn it into butter like other girls her age. After a time she would be expected to produce the usual amount and weight of butter like the others.

But being a very thoughtful and kind young woman and wishing to obey God rather than men, she generously gave away all the butter she had made to the poor and homeless.[5] When the time came to hand over the butter she had made, her turn came at last. Her companions had given over their butter, but now it was time for the maiden blessed above all others to produce hers.

She was dreadfully afraid of her mother's anger since she had given away everything she had made to the poor, not thinking of the consequences. But burning brightly with the unquenchable fire of faith, she turned to God and prayed.

God, our helper in time of need, heard the prayers of the maiden because she believed in him. He miraculously restored the butter she needed.[6]

Most holy Brigid showed her mother that there was nothing lacking from her labors. Indeed, she had made more butter than any of her companions. When everyone saw this great miracle with their own eyes, they praised God who had done the deed and marveled at the great faith that dwelled in the heart of the virtuous maiden.

She Takes the Veil

Not long after this, her parents, as is the custom, wished for Brigid to marry a man. But she was inspired by heaven and wished instead to offer herself to God as a chaste virgin, so she went to the most holy bishop Mac Caille of blessed memory. He was impressed by the heavenly longing, modesty, and great love of chastity in the maiden, and so he placed a white veil and shining garment over her saintly head.

Before God and the bishop, Brigid fell humbly to her knees in front of the altar and offered her virginal crown to almighty God. Then she touched the wood at the base of the altar with her hand.

Because of the purity of her touch, that wood is green today as if it had not been cut and stripped of its bark but was still attached to its roots. Even now it cures all the faithful of sickness and disease.

The Dog and the Bacon

I cannot omit recording the story of another miracle performed by that most famous handmaid of God who was ceaselessly devoted to his service. Once when she was cooking bacon in a cauldron for visitors who would be coming soon, she felt sorry for a fawning and begging dog and gave him some.[7] But when the bacon was taken from the cauldron and divided among the guests, there was plenty to eat as if none had been given away. Those who saw this marveled at the girl unmatched in faith and virtue. They spread the story praising a maiden worthy to perform such great deeds.

Harvesting in the Rain

One day Brigid called together reapers and workers to harvest her fields. However, when they arrived, the day of the gathering became thick with clouds and threatened rain.[8] Indeed through the whole province the glens and gullies of the land overflowed with water. Only Brigid's fields remained dry with no hindrance or damage from the torrents of rain that fell. And although workers throughout the province were prevented that day from harvesting grain, her workers, by the power of God, labored from sunrise to sunset that day free of rain and shadow of darkness.

The Cow Milked Three Times in One Day

This miracle deserves to be admired among the many performed by Brigid. One time some bishops came to visit and stay with her, but she did not have enough food for them. But the power of God provided for her needs abundantly, as usual. She milked the same cow three times on a single day, contrary to the natural order of things, so that this animal miraculously produced as much milk as three of the best cows normally would.[9]

Hanging a Cloak on a Sunbeam

Here I must include a miracle to make you rejoice, in which Brigid's pure virginal mind and the helping hand of God came together in one accord.

Once when she was tending her sheep and grazing them in a grassy field, she was soaked by a fierce downpour of rain from the heavens and went into a house wearing her wet clothes. As she entered the dark home, she was blinded by a ray of the sun shining through a small opening. Thinking the beam of light was a slanting tree built into the house, she took off her wet clothes to hang them there. And just as if the ray of sunlight were a solid piece of wood, the clothes remained on top of it.[10]

When the people who owned the home and all their neighbors saw this astonishing miracle, they gave worthy praise to this extraordinary woman.

The Boy Who Stole Seven Sheep

The following miracle must also be mentioned.

Once when holy Brigid was in the field attentively tending her flock of sheep as they fed, a young scoundrel came to her cunningly to test her generosity to the poor. He sought her out seven times that day disguised in different clothes each time and received from her seven wethers which he hid away in secret.[11] And when as usual in the evening the flock was driven to the fold, they were counted two or three times and found to be no less in number than when they had set out that morning.

When those who had helped the lad steal the sheep realized how God had made his power manifest through the maiden, they returned the seven missing sheep to her flock. But even then the number of sheep was neither more nor less than it had been before.

Because of this and countless other miracles, the great fame of this handmaid of God was on the lips of all, not undeservedly, but because she was most excellent and worthy of praise.

Water Turned into Beer

Another miracle performed by worthy Brigid was this.

Lepers came to her asking for beer, although she had none to give.[12] But seeing water prepared for baths, she blessed it with the power of faith and turned it into the finest beer.[13] She then drew it out in abundance for the thirsty lepers.

The one who turned water into wine in Cana of Galilee also changed water into beer through the faith of this most blessed woman.

But having spoken of this miracle, it is right to mention yet another.

The Virginity of a Young Woman Restored

There was a certain young woman who had taken a vow of virginity, but by human weakness had given in to youthful desire and become pregnant, her womb swelling. Brigid, drawing on the most potent strength of her matchless faith, blessed the woman so that the fetus inside her disappeared without childbirth and pain.[14] Thus the young woman became a virgin again and afterward did penance.

And in accord with the saying that all things are possible to those who believe,[15] Brigid worked countless miracles every day with nothing proving impossible for her.

Turning Stone to Salt

Again on a certain day a man came to her seeking salt, just as countless poor and destitute people were accustomed to come to her about their needs. The most blessed Brigid in that hour made salt from a stone which she had blessed and generously gave plenty to the one who had asked.[16] And thus the man rejoiced and returned home again carrying the salt.

Opening the Eyes of the Blind

I think I should also include this most powerful miracle and divine work done by Brigid, who in imitation of the divine power of our Savior performed a truly extraordinary deed.[17] Following the example of our Lord, she opened the eyes of a man born blind.

For the Lord has generously given his power and abilities to his followers. Although he says of himself, "I am the light of the world,"[18] nonetheless he says to his disciples, "You are the light of the world."[19] And about them also he says, "The works which I do, they will do also and greater than these they will do."[20]

Thus the faith of Brigid, like a mustard seed,[21] was so great that she was able to open the pure and shining eyes of one blind by nature from birth in a marvelous act of God.

This woman who performed such great miracles had such a humble heart, pure mind, modest ways, and was so filled with spiritual grace that she acquired great authority in divine worship and gained a name celebrated above all the virgins of her time.

Healing a Mute Girl

One day a woman from outside the community who was a follower of Brigid came to visit her with her twelve-year-old daughter. This girl had not been able to speak from birth. With great reverence the mother bowed to Brigid, as everyone did, and with her head lowered approached to receive a kiss of peace.

As Brigid was friendly and cheerful to all, she conversed with the woman warmly, sprinkling her words with divine salt.[22] Then in the manner of our Savior who ordered the little ones come to him,[23] she took the hand of the young girl in her own. Brigid did not know she was mute and so asked her what she wished to do with her life, whether she wanted to take the holy veil on her head and be a virgin always or to be given in marriage.

The mother spoke up and said her daughter was not able to reply, but Brigid said she would not let go of the girl's hand until she herself spoke. And when the girl was asked a second time, she answered saying, "I wish nothing more than what you want."

And from that day forward, with her mouth opened, her tongue freed, and the chains which had held her fallen away, the young woman was able to speak.[24]

The Dog Who Guarded the Bacon

And who would not be moved by this miracle of Brigid not heard before by the ears of many?

Once when she was intent on her meditation of heavenly things, as was her custom, turning her thoughts from the things of this earth to those greater glories of heaven, she sent a dog away with a piece of bacon. It was a large piece, not at all small. And when they searched for it they found it exactly where the dog was accustomed to stay. A month had passed, but they found the bacon whole and untouched, for the dog had not dared to eat something entrusted to him by the blessed virgin. He had been a patient and proper guardian of the meat, contrary to his own nature. He proved himself tamed and restrained by a divine miracle.[25]

The Unstained Cloak

The miracles of Brigid grew in number daily, so that they can scarcely be counted. How full of compassion and piety she was, giving alms freely to the poor who sought her out whether it was convenient or not.

Once when a certain beggar came and asked her for food, she hurried to those cooking meat so that she might take some back to the man in need.[26] But the servant standing at the cauldron was not very bright and foolishly placed a piece of poorly cooked meat into the fold of her white cloak. Brigid carried it back to the beggar, but her cloak remained unstained and shining white.

The Cow and the Calf

This wonder from her kind works we must also admire.

Many poor people and pilgrims came to her from everywhere drawn by the stories of her miracles and by her great generosity. One of these was an unpleasant leper who demanded that she give him the best cow of the herd along with the best calf. Hearing this request, she did not turn him away, but learned which cow was the best of all and freely gave it to him. Along with this she gave him the best and most beautiful calf, the offspring of a different cow.[27]

She even had such sympathy for the sick man that she placed him in her own chariot for the long journey over the broad plain so that he would not be worn out driving the cow. She also ordered that the calf be placed behind him in the chariot.[28]

The cow licked the calf with her tongue with no one urging it, caring for it as if it were her own, and followed behind the chariot until they reached their destination.[29]

So you see, my dear brothers, that even brute animals obeyed her against their own nature.

The Cattle Thieves

After a time, some most wicked thieves who feared neither God nor man[30] came from another province on a cattle raid. They easily crossed a wide river at a ford and stole the cattle of Brigid.[31]

But on their return journey the same river became a mighty flood from a sudden rain and disrupted their plans. The river rose like a towering wall and did not permit the most wicked theft of holy Brigid's cattle to be carried out. It overwhelmed the thieves and dragged them away.[32] The cattle were freed and with their leather ropes hanging from their horns, they returned to their herd and pen.

The Chariot Pulled by a Single Horse

In the following story the power of God was also made clear.

On a certain day the most holy Brigid, having learned of some pressing need, set out in a two-horse chariot[33] to address an assembly of the people.[34] As she sat in the chariot, she was engaged in contemplative meditation as was her custom, bringing the heavenly life down to earth as she prayed to the Lord.

But coming down a hill at the end of the journey, one of the horses panicked and twisted itself loose from its reins, slipping free of its yoke and running frightened across the plain. The other horse, however, remained in its yoke.

But the hand of God held up the yoke on the empty side and kept it from falling as the whole assembled crowd watched this testimony of divine power. Meanwhile, Brigid continued to pray peacefully in the chariot as she was pulled without difficulty to the meeting by a single horse. Thus confirming her teaching by signs and wonders,[35] she addressed the people with helpful words sprinkled with divine salt.

Taming a Wild Boar

I believe this miracle of Brigid should also be included.

Once a single wild boar of the forest fled terrified into the middle of a herd of pigs belonging to blessed Brigid.[36] But she saw him in the herd and blessed him so that he became unafraid like one of her own and was content to remain with them.[37]

So you see, my brothers, that even the wild animals and beasts were not able to resist her words and wishes, but became tame and subject to her will.

Wolves as Swineherds

Once there was a certain man who came to Brigid among the others bringing gifts to her. He arrived from a distant province and offered her fat pigs, asking only that she send some men with him to his farm located three or four days across the broad plain so that she could receive the animals from him. Brigid agreed and dispatched the men with him as companions.

After they had traveled a single day they came to a mountain near these regions called Gabor. There they saw coming toward them the man's own pigs, which they had thought were far away, being driven forward by wolves. When they were closer, the man saw for certain that they were his pigs and that they were being driven by wild wolves.[38] These animals from the deep forests and broad plains of the Liffe were laboring as faithful swineherds because of their great respect for blessed Brigid.

When they came to the men, the wolves left them unharmed, acting with great intelligence and contrary to their nature. And thus the next day the men who had been sent by Brigid arrived home, telling of this wondrous deed.

The King and the Fox

Again I must not pass over another wondrous story of Brigid.

One day a certain ignorant man saw a fox walking through the palace of a king.[39] Because he was foolish, he thought it was a wild fox, not knowing that it was in fact a familiar animal in the court beloved by the ruler as it was able to do many tricks with great agility and cleverness for him and his nobles.

In the sight of everyone, the man killed the fox. The people of the court were horrified and bound him to lead him before the king, who was so furious when he heard what had happened that he declared that unless the man produced another fox that was able to do all the tricks of the previous animal, he would order his death. He would also seize the wife and children of the man and turn them into slaves.

When holy and esteemed Brigid learned what had happened, she was moved with great pity and holy compassion. She ordered that her chariot be yoked and set off across the plain to the royal palace. As she traveled along the road, she prayed earnestly to the Lord, pouring forth the sorrow in her heart for the unfortunate man who had been unjustly condemned. The Lord heard her ceaseless prayers and without delay sent one of his own wild foxes to meet her on her journey. The animal came bounding across the plain and jumped into Brigid's chariot, hiding itself under her cloak as it rode tamely along with her.

When she came to the king, she began to beseech him to release the poor, ignorant fellow and free him from his chains. But the ruler would not listen to her prayers and insisted that he would not free the man unless he received another fox as tame and talented as the one he had before.

Then before the eyes of the crowd, Brigid pulled out the fox hiding under her cloak. This animal performed all the tricks of his predecessor with the subtlety and skill of the previous fox. When the king saw this, he was overjoyed and all his nobles burst into loud applause as the creature finished its tricks. The king ordered that the chains of the condemned man be removed and he be set free.

Having accomplished her mission, Brigid set off again to her home. The fox, meanwhile, broke away and dashed quickly through the crowd, weaving cleverly through the legs of the onlookers. It ran from the court and returned safely to its own home in the forest with a crowd of horsemen and hounds chasing it all the way.

Everyone greatly admired this miracle of Brigid and venerated the blessed woman capable of such impressive wonders that grew ever greater.

The Wild Ducks

One day when blessed Brigid saw some ducks swimming in the water and flying through the air as such birds naturally do, she called to them to come to her. The ducks came at the sound of her voice with a great desire to obey, not fearing to put themselves in her care.

She touched them with her hand and embraced them for some time until she again allowed them to fly away and return to where they were before. Through his visible creatures Brigid praised the invisible creator of all things, to whom, as one has said, all living things are subject and for whom all things live.[40]

From these deeds everyone may clearly understand that all the creatures of nature—whether wild beasts, cattle, or birds—were subject to her will.

The Murderers Who Killed a Phantom

This miracle of Brigid must be repeated to the ears of the faithful and be celebrated for all ages to come.

Once when Brigid was sowing the life-giving seeds of the Lord's word among all listeners,[41] as was her usual way, she saw nine men wearing the costumes of their particular foolish and diabolical superstition. They were making ridiculous noises that matched well the great madness of their minds. Their path was one of sorrow and unhappiness—the way of the ancient master who ruled over them. They were thirsting for blood and had made a most wicked vow that before the beginning of the next month they would commit murder and butchery.

The most reverent and kindly Brigid spoke to them with many calming words that they might realize the deadly error of their crimes and turn their hearts from the path of damnation they had chosen. But because of their madness, they said they would not change their ways until they had completed the vows they had made. But the renowned virgin continued to beseech them, pouring forth prayers to God since, like the Lord himself, she wished that all people would come to the knowledge of the truth.

So when the evil men left her, they seemed to see the person they desired to kill. They stabbed him repeatedly with their spears and cut off his head with a sword. Then as if in a triumphal parade over a hated enemy, they marched back with their weapons covered in blood and gore for everyone to see.

But the miracle is that they had killed no one at all, although they believed they had fulfilled their vows. Since there was nobody missing from that province and no doubt about what had actually happened, the wonder of the divine gift having been accomplished by holy Brigid became known to all. And the men who had been murderers before turned their hearts in repentance to the Lord.

The Hungry Man

In the following miracle the divine power of God was made manifest through blessed Brigid in an amazing act of sacred faith.

Once there was a man named Lugaid who was the strongest and most powerful of all men. He was so strong he could lift as much as twelve laborers all by himself when he wished, but he also had such a large appetite that he ate as much as a dozen men every day. Since his ravenous hunger equaled his abilities, he asked Brigid if she would pray to the Lord to take away his excessive appetite without reducing his strength.

And thus Brigid blessed the man and prayed to God for him. Afterward Lugaid was content to eat only as much as a single man, but he retained the strength of twelve men and was as powerful as before.

Moving a Giant Tree

Among her famous miracles is this outstanding and excellent work, which I ought to make known to everyone.

There was a certain tree, grand and magnificent, which had been prepared and cut down by skilled woodsmen of the forest.

Because of its great size a large number of strong men had come together to move it from the very difficult place where it had fallen with a crash of its branches. To transport it to its final destination, they had brought many oxen and much equipment for the task. But neither the large crowd of men nor the strength of the oxen nor the multitude of tools could even begin to drag the tree away. So all the men gave up.

But blessed Brigid—with the faith like a mustard seed that our heavenly master teaches us in the words of the gospel can move mountains[42]—enabled the men without any difficulty to lift that tree and bring it to the destination she desired solely by the grace of angels and divine intervention.

And the news of this amazing miracle of God spread throughout all the provinces.

The Lustful Layman and the Silver Brooch

It seems to me that I also cannot pass over the following miracle in silence among the countless others that the venerable Brigid performed.

Once there was a layman who was of noble birth but deceitful in his ways. He burned with lust for a certain young woman and shrewdly planned how he might have sex with her. He decided to entrust a precious silver brooch to her for safekeeping, which he would then secretly steal back and throw into the sea. Then when she was not able to return the brooch, he would demand that she become his slave in recompense so that he might use her as he wished.[43]

He carried out his wicked plan and declared that he would accept nothing except the return of his silver brooch or she must become his slave to use to satisfy his most disgraceful desires.

The chaste maiden fled to holy Brigid as to the safest city of refuge.[44] Brigid listened to her story and was contemplating what to do when, even before they had finished speaking, a man came in bringing fish he had caught in the river. When he had cut the fish open and removed their entrails, suddenly he discovered in the middle of one of them that same silver brooch which the evil man had thrown into the sea.[45]

Thus with a confident spirit the young woman went out with the brooch to an assembly of the people with her wicked accuser to be tried for theft. But she produced the silver brooch for all to see with many who knew the piece of jewelry testifying that it was none other than the same brooch she had been given earlier.

The chaste maiden was set free from the hands of the cruel tyrant, who came to blessed Brigid with head bowed and confessed his crime. The holy woman gave thanks and offered all the glory to God for this great miracle, then went back to her own home.

The Calf and the Loom

I should also include this wonderful and glorious miracle of Brigid, which occurred when she was a guest of a faithful woman.

One day holy Brigid was making a journey according to God's will across the broad plain of Brega. When evening came, she stopped at a woman's hut to spend the night. The woman graciously welcomed her with open hands and took her in as if she were Christ himself,[46] giving thanks to all-powerful God that the most revered Brigid had come to her door.

But because of her poverty, the woman had no wood for a fire or food to put on her table to feed such a guest. Therefore she kindled a fire with the wood of her loom on which she did her weaving.[47] For food she killed the calf of her own cow and roasted it over the flames.[48] All this she did with grateful joy.

When they had eaten dinner with thanks to God and passed the hours of the night in the usual way, the woman who had previously had nothing to offer her holy guest and had killed the calf of her cow to feed her, rose in the morning and found another calf of the same kind with her cow. This animal loved the new calf as much as the old. The woman also found a new loom in her hut of the same quality as the one she had burned.

And so with this pleasing miracle having been accomplished, holy Brigid bade farewell to the house and woman and went once again on her happy way.

The Lepers and the Silver Cup

This famous work is another of Brigid's many miracles that ought to be admired.

Once three sick and suffering lepers came to her asking if she might give them some gift, so she presented them with a silver cup.[49] In order that there might be no discord or contention among them if they divided it among themselves, she ordered a man skilled in weighing gold and silver to cut it into three equal parts. He began to make excuses saying there was no way he could divide it equally, so Brigid grabbed the cup and threw it against a rock and broke it, as she intended, into three equal and identical parts.

The miraculous nature of this action was then shown when the parts were weighed and it was discovered that of the three pieces, none was greater or less than the other, not even by the smallest amount.

And so the poor sick men had no cause for hard feelings among themselves and happily returned home together.

The Vestments of the Bishop

The following story shows that Brigid, just like most blessed Job,[50] never sent away a poor man empty-handed.

Once she gave away to the poor the vestments of the exalted and eminent Bishop Conlaed.[51] These vestments had been brought from across the sea and were used for the solemnities of the Lord[52] and the vigils of the Apostles[53] when he offered the sacred mysteries on the altar and in the sanctuary.[54]

When the time of the solemnity arrived, as was customary for the pontifex of the people, he was preparing to dress in his usual raiment. But since holy Brigid had already given away his episcopal vestments to Christ who had come to her in the appearance of a poor man, she substituted other vestments of equal texture and color, which had just been given to her by Christ whom she had clothed as a pauper. These vestments were brought to her in a two-wheeled chariot.

Just as she had freely offered the vestments to the poor, so she was given new ones in place of these when she needed them most. For since she herself was a living and most blessed member of body with Christ as its head, she had the power to perform every miracle she desired.

Honey for a Poor Man

This is another miraculous work of Brigid, which cannot be passed over.

There was a certain poor man who, compelled by some need, asked her for a small amount of honey.[55] Brigid was so sorry she had no honey to give the one who was asking, but then she heard a hum of bees underneath the floor of the house where she was staying. When the place where she heard the bees was dug up and searched, she found enough honey for the man who had asked. Thus the poor man received the gift of honey from Brigid and he returned rejoicing to his own home.

The River and the Road

Holy Brigid also shines forth in this miracle.

One time the king of the country where she lived issued an edict to all the tribes and provinces under his yoke and rule that all the regions, provinces, people, and tribes were to come together to build a wide and firm road.[56] First they were to lay a foundation of tree branches and sturdy stones in the deep and almost impassable bog and along the swampy places where a large river ran. The road should be able to bear the weight of wagons, horsemen, chariots, carts, crowds, and the rush against enemies from every direction.

The multitude of people came together by clans and families to divide up the sections of road each would have to build so that every group could be assigned an appropriate part. But when the most difficult section of the road next to the river fell by lot to a certain powerful tribe by chance, they did not want to perform such great labor.[57] That wicked and unjust tribe forced the weaker tribe of holy Brigid to build the difficult section of the road and took a length for themselves away from the river.

Then the people of holy Brigid by birth, beaten down by the stronger tribe and without any hope of recourse, came to her for help. But it is said that Brigid told them, "Go! God has the will and the power to make the river move from the place where you labor so hard to the section which the other tribe has taken for themselves."

And the next morning when her tribe arose to work on the road by the river that troubled them so, they saw the stream had moved from its ancient course between two banks to the section taken by the powerful and bullying tribe which had compelled the smaller and weaker people of holy Brigid to labor harshly and unjustly.

As proof of this miracle, even today the remnants of that river with its empty banks once brimming and rushing with water can be seen, though dry now without any flow of water at all.

The Millstone

Brigid not only worked miracles when she was in the flesh, but even after she died she made manifest many wonders by the grace of God in her own monastery where her venerable body lies. I have not only heard of these but have seen them with my own eyes.

Once there was an abbot of the greatest and most famous monastery of holy Brigid—which I briefly mentioned earlier in this little book—who ordered workers and stonecutters to seek out and cut a millstone from the rock wherever they might find it and bring it back to the monastery.[58] The men set out without knowledge of the difficulty of the path they were taking and climbed to the summit of a rocky mountain.[59] There they found a great mass of rock and from it cut a round and shaped millstone.

When this task was complete, the abbot from the monastery came to the mountain with some oxen.[60] But the animals were not able to climb to the summit on account of the steep slope and even the abbot could scarcely reach the top with the few men who followed him.

The abbot, along with his companions and all the workers, tried to think of some way they might move this huge millstone from the peak of the high mountain, for there was no way the oxen could be yoked to pull the stone on that steep path. Soon they gave up, saying they would have to leave the millstone that the workers had labored in vain to cut. But the faithful abbot with wisdom and prudence said to the workers, "We cannot abandon hope. Lift up the stone with all your might and roll it down the slope of the mountain. We cannot do this by our own skill and strength, but by the name and power of holy Brigid we can move it from this rocky and difficult place to where the oxen can drag it. Only Brigid can do that, for nothing is impossible for her, since scripture that says everything is possible to one who believes."

And so with firm faith they lifted and pushed the stone until it was rolling slowly down the mountain all by itself. Sometimes it swerved away from rocks and other times it jumped over them. Then it rolled through swampy ground at the bottom of the mountain on which neither men nor oxen could stand. It made its miraculous journey down the mountain to the plain with the men behind without breaking at all so that it came to the place where the oxen were waiting. And thus the beasts dragged it from there to the mill where the craftsmen skillfully joined it to a second stone.

And so the millstone which had been moved by the name of blessed Brigid became known to everyone and this previously unknown miracle was added to her glory.

But once there was a certain pagan druid who lived in a house near the mill. He deviously sent his grain to the mill with some simpleton, so that the miller who ground the grain would not know whose it was.

When the miller poured the man's grain into the mill, the stone would not move, no matter the force of the flowing water or the efforts of the workers to make it move as it always did.

The men at the mill who saw this were totally perplexed and frustrated until they discovered that the grain belonged to the druid. Then they had no doubt that the millstone in which holy Brigid had worked such a miracle was refusing to grind the grain of the pagan man into flour. But as soon as they took out the grain of the druid and replaced it with grain from the monastery, the normal motion of the millstone was immediately restored without any difficulty.

After some time it happened that this mill was ravaged by fire. It was then again that no small miracle occurred, for the building was totally consumed by flames destroying everything, including the other stone, but the millstone that was sacred to holy Brigid alone was not damaged in the great fire.

After this miracle the millstone was carried to the monastery where it was fixed in a place of honor next to the decorated gate of the wall around the church. Many people gather there to venerate the miracles of holy Brigid. The stone drives out diseases and sicknesses from the faithful who touch this stone of Brigid, who performed the miracles mentioned above.

The Church Door

Finally, I cannot keep silent about a miracle which happened while repairing the church where the glorious bodies of Archbishop Conlaed and the most flourishing virgin Brigid rest, one on the right and one on the left of the decorated altar. They lie in tombs ornamented with every kind of gold, silver, and gems of precious stones with crowns of gold and silver hanging above. Around them are various images with carvings in many colors.[61]

In an ancient place something new has been born. Into this church decorated with painted images and with its spacious floor and towering roof, a growing number of men and women have come. The grand church has three large sections marked by wooden partitions under one roof. The first partition, which is decorated with pictures and cloth hangings, stretches across the whole eastern front of the church from one wall to the other. There are two openings in this front partition. Through the opening on the right the archbishop enters with the monks and those who celebrate the sacred mysteries to offer the holy and divine sacrifice. Through the other opening on the left, only the abbess enters with her nuns and faithful widows to partake of the banquet of Christ's body and blood.

The second partition on the floor of the church splits it into two sections from the western end to the partition at the front. There are many windows in these two sections. There is also one decorated door in the right section through which the priests and all the men of the congregation enter into the church. In the left section another door allows entrance to the virgins and the faithful women of the church. Thus in one grand basilica the whole people of all ranks, social standing, sex, and place of origin gather together to praise almighty God in one spirit, though they are of different standing in the world.

Once when the old door of the left entryway—where holy Brigid used to come into the church—was hung on its hinges by the workmen, it was discovered that it was not large enough to fill the new doorway. The whole bottom quarter of the entryway showed an open gap. Only if another quarter had been added to the door would it have then filled up the space in the new entryway.

The craftsmen were trying to decide whether they should make a whole new door to fill up the entryway or simply attach enough wood to the bottom of the old door to cover the gap. But then a very learned man who was the greatest of all the craftsmen in Ireland offered his prudent advice. He said they should pray during the coming night at the tomb of holy Brigid so that she might reveal to them in the morning what it was that she wanted them to do about the door. And so he spent the night meditating at the resting place of glorious Brigid.

When morning came after the prayers were said, the craftsman hung the old door back on its hinges and closed it. It now fit perfectly being neither too large nor too small in size. And so Brigid had made the door bigger so that it filled the entryway and there was no gap visible except when it was pulled back on its hinges to enter the church. This miracle of God's power was clearly revealed to the eyes of everyone who saw that door and doorway.

Who can express in words the great beauty of this church and the countless wonders of the city around it, if it is right to call it a city even though it doesn't have walls surrounding it?[62] Nonetheless it is called a vast and metropolitan city because of the many people who gather there. Holy Brigid marked out the area around it with a boundary so that it fears no human foe. It is the safest of all the cities of refuge in Ireland for those who flee to it. Kings keep secure their treasures there at that most exalted place.

Who can count the people who come there from all the provinces of Ireland? Some come for the feasts, others for the spectacle of the crowds. Still others come to be healed of their diseases, while others come bearing great gifts and dedications at the celebration of the feast of holy Brigid, which is on the first day of February,[63] the day she fell asleep and cast off the burdens of the flesh to follow the lamb of God into the heavenly mansions.

EPILOGUE

And so I ask forgiveness from my brothers reading these words and even from those emending them. I was compelled to write this book out of obedience. I have no special knowledge and have only skimmed over an immense sea of stories about holy Brigid— a corpus of stories daunting even to the most learned of men. I have recorded in my rustic speech only a few of her countless and wonderful miracles.[64]

I am Cogitosus. Pray for me, a sinful descendant of Áed. I ask that you commend me to the Lord with your prayers and that God might hear you who follow the peace of the gospel.

THE VOYAGE OF SAINT BRENDAN

The Voyage of Saint Brendan was written by an unknown author sometime in the ninth century. It tells the story of an abbot from three centuries earlier voyaging across the sea in search of a heavenly land promised by God to the saints. Along the way Brendan and his band of intrepid monks encounter holy men, sea monsters, talking birds, and many other creatures and characters both benevolent and threatening. Brendan faithfully leads his monks as they live the monastic life sailing the ocean while observing the daily prayers and services and the seasons of the church year.

Some have tried to find in the spiritual voyage of Brendan a record, however garbled, of actual journeys to the distant islands of the North Atlantic and even to America. We know from other sources that Irish monks did indeed travel at least as far as Iceland in search of spiritual retreats. Lacking the desert wastelands to which their Christian brothers and sisters of Egypt and the Middle East withdrew, many of the monks of Ireland chose instead to make their homes on inhospitable islands off the Irish coast or even farther away. But whatever merits the work may have as a record of such distant journeys, the *Voyage* is above all an allegory of the Christian life. The crystal mountain Brendan discovers may have been based on an iceberg and the fiery mountain of the tale may originate in a volcanic eruption in Iceland, but to focus on such details is to miss the point of the story. For medieval Christian readers, the voyage was a spiritual journey in the dangerous and unpredictable seas of life, in which, as Brendan says, one must sometimes unfurl the sails and let God lead his servants where he wishes.

The Voyage of Saint Brendan is part of an ancient tradition of travel and adventure stories that goes back to Homer's *Odyssey* and Virgil's *Aeneid*. There were probably similar native Irish stories long before the arrival of Christianity which influenced Brendan's tale. The earlier *Voyage of Bran*, for example, tells of an Irish band of sailors led by the hero Bran who sail to strange and wondrous islands in search of a land of paradise. Such stories were popular in early Ireland, as were tales of the Tír na nÓg, the land of youth, which lay far to the west. Standing on the cliffs of western Ireland and gazing out beyond the crashing waves at the endless ocean, modern visitors can easily see why the Irish were fascinated by and told stories of what lay beyond the horizon.

The Voyage of Saint Brendan stirred the popular imagination far beyond Ireland and became a medieval bestseller throughout western Europe, with translations in languages as diverse as French, Italian, English, German, and Norwegian. For readers today, as far as we may be from the lives of monks and sea monsters, the story is still a moving and magical journey.

The Latin text of the voyage with commentary is in Carl Selmer, *Navagatio Sancti Brendani Abbatis*.

Two translations with useful introductions are John J. O'Meara's *The Voyage of Saint Brendan* and J. F. Webb's *The Age of Bede*, 233–267.

A very helpful collection of essays about Brendan and his voyage is Jonathan Wooding, *The Otherworld Voyage in Early Irish Literature*.

THE TALE OF BARRIND

Holy Brendan, the son of Findlug and descendant of Alte of the Eogan people, was born in the bogs of Munster. He was a man of great abstinence and famous for his miracles, the spiritual father of almost three thousand monks.

Once when he was struggling with himself in a place called the Meadow of the Miracle of Brendan, a certain priest named Barrind, a kinsman of his, came to him in the evening.

After Brendan had asked him many questions, Barrind began to cry and fell flat on the ground, remaining there a long time in prayer. But holy Brendan raised him up from the earth and kissed him, saying:

> *"Father, why should we be sorrowful at your arrival? Didn't you come here to comfort us? You ought instead to*

> bring great joy to the brothers. Speak to us the word of
> God and restore our spirits with news of the many won-
> ders you saw on the ocean."

When holy Brendan had finished speaking, holy Barrind began to
talk about a certain island, saying:

> "My dear son Mernoc, a steward of Christ's poor, left me
> as he wished to become a hermit. He discovered an island
> near a rocky mountain called the Island of Delight. After
> a long time, I heard that he had many monks with him
> and that God had worked many miracles through him, so
> I set out to visit my dear son.
>
> "When I arrived after a three-day journey, Mernoc
> hurried out with his brothers to meet me, for the Lord
> had revealed to him that I was coming. So as we were
> sailing to the island, a multitude of brothers came
> swarming out to meet us from their cells like bees from a
> hive. They all slept in scattered dwelling places, but they
> lived as one in faith, hope, and love. They dined at a
> common table and always came together for the work of
> God. They ate nothing except fruit, nuts, roots, and other
> types of plants. After evening prayers, each monk would
> remain in his individual cell until the cock crowed or the
> bell was rung.
>
> "And so I stayed the night and walked around the
> island with my dear son Mernoc until he brought me to

the western shore, where there was a little boat. Then he said to me:

"'Father, let's get into the boat and sail away westward to the island called the Land Promised to the Saints—a place God will give to our successors at the end of the age.'

"We climbed in and sailed away, but soon such a fog began to surround us that we were scarcely able to see the bow or the stern of our boat. Then after about an hour, a great light shone round about us and we saw a spacious land, green and fruitful.When the boat reached the shore we got out and walked around the island for fifteen days without ever reaching the end of it. Every plant we saw had flowers and all the trees bore fruit, while the stones of that land were all precious. At last on the fifteenth day we discovered a river flowing from the east to the west. We considered all these things, but were in doubt about what we should do next. It seemed best to cross the river, but we waited for God to lead us.

"While we were waiting, a man suddenly appeared before us clothed in light. He called us by name and greeted us, saying:

"'Rejoice, good brothers, for the Lord himself has revealed this land to you, a land he will give to his saints. This river marks the middle of the island, but you may not pass to the other side. Return therefore from where you came.'

"When he had said this, I immediately asked him where he came from and what his name was. He answered me:

"'Why do you ask me from where I come or what I am called? Why don't you ask me instead about this island? Just as you see it now, it has been since the beginning of the world. While you have been here, have you needed food or drink or clothing? Yet a whole year you have passed here on this island not eating or drinking. Neither have you needed sleep nor has night fallen. For our Lord Jesus is the light of this place.'[1]

"With this man we started back right away until we came to the shore where our boat lay waiting. As we set out in our little craft, the man vanished from our sight and we were surrounded by fog until we came again to the Island of Delight. The brothers saw us arriving and shouted with great joy at our return. They grieved at our long absence, saying:

"'Why, fathers, did you abandon your sheep to wander without nourishment in these woods? We knew that our abbot frequently went away from us to go to some place, but we never knew where. But then he was only gone for a month or perhaps two weeks or a week or even less.'

"When I heard this, I began to comfort them, saying:

"'Think, brothers, only of good in this matter. You live without a doubt at the very gates of paradise. This home of yours is near the island called the Land Promised to the Saints, where there is no night but only day. That is where your abbot Mernoc goes so often with an angel of the Lord to guide him. Can't you tell by the smell of our clothes that we have been in the paradise of God?'

"Then the brothers answered, saying:

"'Father, we knew that you were in the paradise of God out on the sea, but we do not know where that place is. For often we have smelled the lingering odor of paradise on the garments of our abbot for forty days after he has returned.'

"I stayed there with my dear son Mernoc for two weeks neither eating nor drinking, but to those around us our bodies seemed as satisfied as if we were full of new wine. Then after forty days I received the blessing of the brothers and the abbot and set off with my companions to return to my cell, which I will go to tomorrow."

When they had heard these words, holy Brendan and his whole community fell down to the ground in worship, glorifying God and saying:

"The Lord is just in all his ways and holy in all his works, for he has revealed to his servants so many great and wondrous miracles. Blessed is he in his gifts who has refreshed us this day with such spiritual food."[2]

When these words were spoken, holy Brendan said, "Let us go now to renew the body and to follow the new commandment."[3]

When the night had passed and morning had come, Barrind received the blessings of the brothers and returned to his own cell.

THE MEETING OF THE MONKS

Holy Brendan therefore selected fourteen brothers from his whole community and went with them together into an oratory, closing the door behind him.[4] He then spoke to them, saying:

> *"My most beloved fellow warriors, I seek your counsel and advice. For my desire and all my thoughts have come together into one purpose—if it is the will of God, I plan to seek out with all my heart the Land Promised to the Saints spoken of by Father Barrind. How does this seem to you? What counsel do you give?"*

When they had heard the plan of their holy father, they answered him together, saying:

> *"Father, your will and ours are one. Haven't we left behind our parents?[5] Haven't we set aside our inheritance? Haven't we given our bodies into your hands? Therefore we are ready to go with you whether unto death or life. We seek only one thing—the will of God."*

SAINT ENDA

Holy Brendan and those with him decided to fast for forty days—but only for three days at a time—and then set out on their voyage.[6] When the forty days were completed, they bade farewell to the monks and Brendan left one of them in charge of the monastery, the same man who would later be his successor there. He sailed west with the fourteen brothers to visit the island of a certain holy father named Enda.[7] They stayed there for three days and three nights.

BUILDING THE BOAT

After Brendan had received the blessing of the holy father and all the monks who were with him, he set out into a distant part of the region where he had grown up and where his parents lived, although he did not wish to visit them. He pitched a tent there on a certain headland that stretches out far into the sea at a place now called Brendan's Seat where there is only enough room to launch one boat.

Holy Brendan and those with him began to build a very light craft there with iron tools.[8] The ribs and frame of the boat were made of wood, as is usual in those lands. They covered it with cowhides tanned with oak bark, then greased all the seams where the hides joined with fat. They placed in the craft enough skins to make two more boats, along with supplies for forty days, fat for treating the hides, and other necessities for human life. At last they fixed a wooden mast in the middle of the boat with a sail and other equipment for steering the craft.

Holy Brendan then ordered his monks in the name of the Father and the Son and the Holy Spirit to enter the boat.

THREE LATE ARRIVALS

While Brendan was standing alone on the shore and blessing the place they would launch the boat, suddenly three brothers arrived who had followed him from his monastery. They immediately fell down at the feet of the holy man, saying:

> *"Father, please let us sail with you wherever you may go*
> *or we will die here of hunger and thirst. For we have de-*
> *cided to be wandering pilgrims all the days of our lives."*

When the man of God saw their distress, he ordered them into the boat, saying, "Let your will be done, my sons."

But then he added:

> *"I know why you have come. One of you brothers has done*
> *something worthy and God has prepared a most suitable*
> *place for him. But for the other two he will prepare a ter-*
> *rible judgment."*

THE MYSTERIOUS ISLAND

Holy Brendan then climbed into the boat. The men raised the sails and began to steer westward toward the summer solstice. They had a favorable wind behind them so they needed to do nothing more than set the sails.

After fifteen days the wind ceased, so the monks took up their oars and rowed until they were exhausted. Holy Brendan began to comfort and encourage them, saying:

> "Brothers, be not afraid. For God himself is our helper, our navigator, and our helmsman to guide us. Bring in the oars and the rudder. Unfurl the sails and let God lead his servants and his ship where he wishes."

And so they sailed on, eating a meal every evening. Sometimes a wind arose, but they were never sure from which direction it came or where it was blowing them.

When forty days had passed and all their food had been eaten, a high and rocky island appeared in the north. After they drew near they saw soaring cliffs like a wall and many small streams pouring down into the sea from the top of the island. But they were not able to find a place to land the boat. The monks were tormented by lack of food and water, so some of them took little vessels and tried to catch the water coming down. But when holy Brendan saw this he said:

> "Stop! You're doing a foolish thing. God does not yet wish to show us a place to land and you would plunder this island? In three days the Lord Jesus Christ will reveal to his servants a place where we can land and refresh our weary bodies."

When they had sailed around the island for three days, about three o'clock in the afternoon on the third day they found a landing place just big enough for a single boat. Holy Brendan immediately stood up and blessed the place. There were towering cliffs of sheer rock like walls on both sides. When everyone had climbed out and stood at last on land, holy Brendan ordered that no one take anything from the boat.

As they were walking along the shore, a dog ran up to them on the path and came to the feet of holy Brendan just as dogs will do with their masters. Then holy Brendan said to the brothers, "Hasn't God sent a fine messenger to us? Let's follow him." And so holy Brendan and his brothers followed the dog to a settlement.

When they entered the place, they saw a great hall lined with beds and seats and with water to wash their feet. But as they sat down, holy Brendan gave these orders to his companions:

> *"Take care, brothers, that Satan lead you not into temp-*
> *tation. For I see that he will tempt one of the brothers who*
> *followed us late from the monastery to commit a most*
> *wicked theft. Pray for his soul, for his flesh has been*
> *handed over to the power of Satan."*

The walls of the house where they were staying were lined with vessels of various metals hanging from the ceiling, along with bridles and horns covered with silver.

Then holy Brendan said to the brother who was accustomed to serve them meals, "Bring the meal which God has prepared for us."

The man immediately jumped up and found a table prepared with linen and set with loaves of wondrous white bread, along with fish. When all was brought before him, holy Brendan blessed the meal and said to the brothers, "Let us thank the God of heaven who gives food to all flesh."

The brothers sat down in their chairs and glorified God. They also had as much to drink as they wanted.

When the meal was over and the worship of God complete, holy Brendan said to them:

> *"Sleep now. Behold, a well-made bed is here for each of*
> *you. It is right that you should all rest your weary bodies*
> *worn out from so much labor."*

But when the brothers had gone to bed, holy Brendan saw the devil at work. He was in the form of a small Ethiopian child with a bridle in his hand and was playing before the face of the brother mentioned before.

Immediately holy Brendan got up and began to pray, staying on his knees all through the night until morning. Then the brothers arose and quickly said the morning service, after which they started to go to the boat. But suddenly a table appeared before them furnished just as the day before. Thus for three days and three nights God prepared a meal for his servants.

THE STOLEN BRIDLE

After this, holy Brendan made ready to leave with his brothers and said to them, "See that none of you takes anything of value from this island."

And they all answered, "God forbid, father, that we should desecrate our voyage with an act of theft."

Then holy Brendan said:

> *"Behold now your brother, the one I spoke of yesterday. He*
> *is hiding a silver bridle close to him which a devil gave to*
> *him last night."*

When he heard these words, that brother threw the bridle away and fell down at the feet of the man of God, saying:

> *"I have sinned, Father. Forgive me. Pray for my soul lest I*
> *perish."*

Immediately all the other monks threw themselves on the ground and prayed to the Lord for the soul of their brother.

After the brothers stood up again and the holy father had helped the sinner to his feet, behold they all saw a little Ethiopian leap from him and cry loudly,[9] saying, "Why, man of God, do you cast me out of my home where I have lived for seven years and deprive me of my inheritance?"[10]

Holy Brendan said to him, "I command you in the name of the Lord Jesus Christ not to harm anyone else until the Day of Judgment."

Then the man of God turned to the sinful monk and said:

> *"Receive the body and blood of the Lord, for your spirit is*
> *about to leave your body. This island will be the place of*

*your tomb. But the brother who came with you from our
monastery will have his tomb in hell."*

And so after the monk had accepted the Eucharist, his spirit left his
body. The brothers watched as his soul was taken up by angels of light.
His body, however, was buried in that place as the holy father said.

FOOD FOR THE JOURNEY

Finally the brothers went with holy Brendan to the shore of the
island where their boat was waiting. While they were getting into
it, a young man ran up to them carrying a basket of bread and a jar
of water. He said to them:

*"Take this blessing from the hand of your servant. A long
journey remains ahead of you before you find rest. But you
will not lack for bread or water from this day until Easter."*

They took the gift and sailed away into the ocean. They ate every
two days as their boat was carried here and there across the sea.

THE ISLAND OF SHEEP

One day they saw an island not far away from them. As they
began to steer toward it, a favorable wind arose to help them.

When the boat reached a landing place, the man of God ordered everyone to go ashore, while he got out after them. As they walked around the island, they discovered many springs and streams full of fish. Then holy Brendan said to the brothers:

> "Let us perform the divine service here and sacrifice to God
> the spotless victim. For today is Maundy Thursday."[11]

And they remained there until Holy Saturday.[12]

Walking around the island, they saw many flocks of sheep, all of the same color, a shining white. They could scarcely see the ground because of the multitude of sheep. Holy Brendan called the brothers together and said to them, "Take what we need from the flock for our feast."

And so the brothers hurried to the flock as the man of God had said and took a single sheep. When they had tied it by the horns, the animal followed the man leading it with a rope in his hand as if it were tame. He came to the place where the man of God stood waiting. The man of God then spoke to the brother and said, "Take an unblemished lamb from the flock."[13] So he hastened and did as he was told.

When they had prepared everything for the service on the next day, a man suddenly appeared to them holding in his hand a basket full of bread baked under coals along with everything else they needed. After he had placed this before the man of God, he fell flat on his face three times before the feet of the holy father, saying, "How am I worthy, O pearl of God, that you should eat on these holy days the work of my hands?"

Holy Brendan lifted him up from the earth and gave him a kiss, saying, "My son, our Lord Jesus Christ led us to this place that we might celebrate his holy resurrection."

And the man said:

> "Father, you will celebrate Holy Saturday here, but the vigils and masses of Easter you will celebrate tomorrow on that island God has shown to you and you see nearby."

After he had said these things, he began to serve the servants of God and to prepare everything for the next day. When the work was completed and all had been carried to the boat, the man said to holy Brendan.

> "Your little boat is not able to carry any more. I will bring to you in eight days everything that you need, food and drink to last until Pentecost."[14]

Holy Brendan said, "How do you know where we will be in eight days?"

And the man said:

> "This night you will arrive at that island you see and stay there until midday tomorrow. After that you will sail westward to another nearby island. It is called the Paradise of Birds. You will remain there until eight days after Pentecost."

Holy Brendan also asked the man how the sheep on the island got to be so big, for they were larger than cattle. And he replied:

> "There is no one to milk the sheep on this island nor is there any winter to distress them. They remain in their pastures day and night. Therefore they are bigger than the sheep in your country."

And so they got into their boat and sailed away, each having blessed the other.

JASCONIUS

When they drew near to the other island, the boat ran aground before it reached the landing place. Holy Brendan ordered the brothers to get out of the boat into the water, and they did so. They pulled the boat with ropes on both sides until they came to the landing place. It was a rocky island without any grass. There were a few pieces of wood on it, but no sand anywhere. All the monks passed the night ashore in prayer while the man of God stayed in the boat. He knew what kind of island it was, but he didn't want to tell them lest they be afraid.

When morning came he told each of the priests to sing Mass, and so they did. Holy Brendan himself sang Mass in the boat while the brothers carried ashore raw meat to salt along with fish they had brought with them from the other island. When they were done, they put a pot of water to boil over a fire. But when they were feeding the fire with wood and the pot began to boil, the island began to move like a wave.[15] The brothers started running to the boat, beseeching the holy father to protect them. One by one he pulled them into the boat and leaving behind everything they had brought to the island, they began to sail away. The island itself moved out into the ocean, while the fire they had lit could be seen for two miles.

Holy Brendan explained this to the monks, saying, "Brothers, do you wonder what this island is?"

And they said, "Yes, indeed, and we are full of fear!"

Then he said to them:

> *"My dear sons, do not be terrified. God revealed the truth about this thing to me last night in a sacred vision. The place where you were is not an island at all, but a fish, the greatest which swims in the ocean. He is always trying to bring his tail to his head, but he cannot since he is so long. His name is Jasconius."*

THE PARADISE OF BIRDS

And when they sailed to that island where they had stayed the three previous nights, they climbed to the highest point of the island facing west. They saw there another island nearby almost joined to the one they were on but separated by a narrow channel.

That island was covered with grass and had many groves of trees along with abundant flowers.

They began to sail around the island looking for a place to land. At last on the southern side they came to a small river flowing into the sea where they came ashore. The monks got out of the boat, but holy Brendan ordered them to pull the craft up the river with ropes with all their might. The river was only as wide as their boat. The father sat in the boat as they hauled it about a mile until they came to the source of the stream. Then holy Brendan said to them, "Behold, our Lord Jesus Christ has given this place to us to remain during the feast of his resurrection." And he added, "Even if we had no other nourishment than this spring, it would be enough. I believe it would provide us with all the food and drink we need."

There was hanging over the spring a tree of surprising girth, but no less amazing in height. It was covered with white birds,[16] so many in fact that it was hard to see the branches or leaves. When the man of God saw these, he began to wonder how so many birds came together in one flock. He was so troubled by this that tears began to pour down his cheeks as he fell to his knees beseeching God, saying:

> *"God, knower of the unknown and revealer of all hidden things, you know the anguish of my heart. I pray to you in your greatness to reveal to me, a sinner, this secret through your great mercy. I ask this not because of any merits or worth I might have, but by your abundant kindness."*

After he had said these things to himself and sat down again, suddenly one of the birds flew down from the tree. Its wings sounded like the ringing of a bell as it settled on the boat across from the man of God. It sat on the highest point of the prow and stretched out its wings as if making a sign of joy. With a peaceful face it gazed at the holy father. Immediately the man of God knew that God had answered his prayer and he said to the bird, "If you are a messenger from God, tell me where all these birds came from and why they are gathered here."

The bird then said:

> "We are from that great destruction of the ancient enemy,[17] but we did not sin with them by our own consent. After we had been created, the fall of that one and his followers ruined us as well. But our God is just and fair. In his judgment he sent us to this place. We are not punished here. We can see the presence of God, but we cannot mingle with those who stood by him. We wander through the many regions of the air and firmament and earth, as do other spirits sent by him. But on holy days and each Sunday we take on the bodies you now see, so that here we may worship and praise our creator. You and your brothers have passed one year on your voyage, but you still have six ahead of you. The place where you celebrated Easter today is where you will celebrate it every year. When that is done, you will find what you seek in your heart—the Land Promised to the Saints."

When it had said these things, the bird took off from the prow of the boat and flew back to the others.

When the hour of evening prayers came, all the birds in the tree began to sing as if with one voice, beating their wings against their sides:

> *"A hymn is due to you, O God, in Zion*
> *and a vow will be paid in Jerusalem."*[18]

They repeated this verse over and over again for about an hour. It seemed to the man of God and to those with him that the chanting and the sound of their wings was like a song of sweet lamentation.

Then holy Brendan said to his brothers, "Refresh your bodies, for today our spirits are full of divine food."

When the meal was finished, they began to celebrate the divine service. When this was done the man of God and those with him gave rest to their bodies until the third hour of the night. The man of God, however, remained awake and roused his brothers to celebrate the vigil of the holy night, beginning with the verse:

> *"Lord, open my lips."*[19]

When the prayer of the holy man was finished, all the birds resounded with wing and voice, singing:

> *"Praise the Lord, all his angels, praise him, all his powers."*[20]

They sang again for a whole hour, just as they had done at evening prayers. Then when dawn shone forth, they began to sing:

"And let the splendor of the Lord be upon us,"[21] using the same rhythm and singing for the same length of time for the psalm as they had in worship at night. Similarly in midmorning prayers they sang this verse:

> *"Sing psalms to our God, sing, sing to our king, sing psalms with wisdom."*[22]

And at noon they sang:

> *"Shine your face on us, O Lord, and have mercy on us."*[23]

And in the midafternoon they sang:

> *"Behold how good and pleasant it is for brothers to live as one."*[24]

And so day and night the birds gave praise to God. Thus holy Brendan refreshed his brothers until eight days after the feast of Easter.

When the days of the feast were completed, he said, "Let us take sustenance from this spring, for so far we have only used it for washing our hands and feet." But as soon as he had said this, behold the man who had stayed with them for three days before Easter and had given them supplies for the feast suddenly arrived with a boat full of food and drink. When everything had been unloaded from the boat, he spoke to the holy father, saying:

> *"Men, brothers, you have enough supplies here to last you until the holy day of Pentecost. Do not drink from this spring, for it is too strong for drinking. I will tell you the nature of this spring. Whoever drinks from it, he will immediately fall into a deep sleep and will not wake up for twenty-four hours. It is only when taken away from the spring that it has the taste and qualities of normal water."*

When the man had received the blessing of the holy father, he returned to his own home.

Holy Brendan remained in that place until eight days before Pentecost, for the singing of the birds revived their spirits. On the day of Pentecost itself, when the holy man had sung the Mass with his brothers, their supplier came again bringing everything they would need for celebrating the feast. When they sat down together to eat, the man spoke to them, saying:

> *"You still have a great journey ahead of you. Fill your vessels with water from the spring and take enough dry bread to eat for a year. I will give you as much as your boat can carry."*

When all this was finished, he accepted a blessing and returned to his own home.

After eight days holy Brendan ordered the boat to be loaded with all the supplies that that man had brought them, along with all the vessels filled with water from the spring. When everything had been brought to the shore, suddenly the same bird as before quickly flew down and sat on the bow of the boat. The man of God could see that it wished to say something to him. Then in a human voice the bird began to speak:

> "You will celebrate the holy day of Easter and the time after the feast with us next year. And where you were for Maundy Thursday, there you will be again next year. Likewise the vigil of the night before Easter you will celebrate as you did before, on the back of Jasconius. Eight months from now you will come to an island called the Island of the Community of Ailbe. There you will celebrate Christmas."

When the bird had said these things, it returned to its own place. Then the brothers unfurled the sails and set off into the ocean. As they did, the birds sang as if with one voice:

> "We praise you, O God, our savior and hope across all boundaries of the earth and the wide sea."[25]

THE COMMUNITY OF AILBE

Then the holy father with his monks were driven this way and that across the wide ocean for three months, seeing nothing but sky and the sea. They ate only every second or third day.

One day at last there appeared to them an island not far away. But as they drew near to the shore, a wind prevented them from landing. For forty days they sailed around the island unable to bring the boat to shore. The brothers who were in the boat began to beseech the Lord with tears begging for his help. Their strength was almost gone and they were very weary.

After three days of fasting and prayer, they found a narrow landing place, large enough only for a single boat. They also saw two springs there, one muddy and the other clear. The brothers rushed to fill their vessels with water, but the man of God looked at them and said:

> *"My sons, do not take anything without the approval of the elders of this island. They will gladly grant you permission to draw the water which you now seek to drink as thieves."*

As they went away from the boat and were considering which part of the island to go to, a very dignified old man with hair like snow and a shining face met them. Three times he fell down on the earth and bowed, embracing the man of God. Holy Brendan and those with him then lifted the man from the ground. After kissing all of them in turn, the old man held the hand of the holy father and led him to a monastery just a short distance away. Holy Brendan stood with his brothers before the gate of the monastery and asked the old man, "Whose monastery is this? Who is in charge here? Where do those who live here come from?"

The holy father asked the old man many questions, but was not able to get any response from him. The man then indicated through gentle signs that he should be silent. When the holy father at last realized this was a place of silence, he warned his brothers, saying, "Guard your tongues from speech lest these brothers be disturbed by your chattering."

When he had said these words, suddenly eleven brothers came to them with boxes of relics and crosses and singings hymns, chanting this verse:

> *"Rise up, holy ones of God, from your homes and seek the way of truth. Sanctify this place, bless your people, and by grace keep your followers in peace."*

When the song was finished, the abbot of the monastery greeted holy Brendan and each of his companions with a kiss. Then the abbot's monks all kissed the brothers of the holy man.

When the kiss of peace had been given all around, they led them into the monastery as is the custom in western lands to lead brothers to prayer. After this the abbot of the monastery and his monks began to wash the feet of their guests and to sing the antiphon:

> *"A new commandment."*

When this was done the abbot led them to the dining room. After a signal was given and hands were washed, he motioned for them to sit down. At the sound of a second signal, one of the brothers of the abbot rose and brought to the table bread that was miraculously white along with roots tasting absolutely wonderful. The monks of the monastery sat mixed with their guests all in order. Every two brothers had a full loaf placed between them. When another signal was sounded, the same brother served them all drink.

The abbot joyously urged the brothers to eat and drink, saying:

> *"This spring which earlier today you wished to drink from secretly, now in love you may drink from openly with joy and fear of the Lord. From that other spring you saw which is muddy, every day the feet of the brothers are washed, for it is always warm. We do not know who bakes the bread you see or who brings it to our kitchen. But we do know that it is given to us his servants by the great kindness of God by means of one of his creatures. We are twenty-four brothers gathered here. Each day we are given twelve loaves of bread to eat, two monks to a loaf. On feast days and on Sundays, God gives a full loaf to each brother so that we have enough left over for supper. Now that you all have arrived, we have been given double the usual amount. Thus Christ has fed us since the time of holy Patrick and holy Ailbe, our father, for eighty years.*[26] *But we never grow old or weak in our limbs. On this island we eat no food prepared by fire, nor does cold or heat overcome us. And when the time for Mass or the vigils*

> *come, the lamps which we brought from our own country*
> *are lit in the church and burn all night, the flame never*
> *diminishing.*

After they had drunk three times, the abbot rang the bell as was his custom. The brothers all solemnly rose together from the table in silence and went ahead of the holy fathers into the church. Holy Brendan and the abbot of the monastery followed them in turn. When they had entered the church, they saw twelve other monks leave the building and bow down quickly to them on their way out. After holy Brendan saw this, he asked, "Abbot, why did these men not eat with us?" And the father said:

> *"Because you all were here and there wasn't enough space*
> *for everyone to eat at the same time. They will eat now*
> *and lack nothing. Meanwhile we will go into the church*
> *and sing evening prayers now so that when those brothers*
> *finish their meal they may come into the church and sing*
> *after us."*

When the evening prayers were finished, holy Brendan began to examine how the church had been built. It was a square as long as it was wide with seven lamps, three in front of the central altar and two before each of the other two altars. The altars were squares made of crystal and the sacred vessels were also of crystal, including the patens,[27] chalices, cruets,[28] and others needed for the divine service. The twenty-four seats that circled the inside of the church were also made of crystal. The seat of the abbot was between the two choirs. One choir would begin and finish with him, as would the other. No one of the monks would dare to begin singing a verse except the abbot. No one in the monastery would speak a word or make any noise. If a monk needed something he would go before the abbot and bow his head to the ground, asking in his heart whatever it was he needed. The abbot would immediately take a tablet and stylus to write down whatever it was that God had revealed to him. He then gave it to the monk who had asked the question.

While holy Brendan was pondering all these things, the abbot said to him, "Father, it is now time for us to return to the dining room so that we might do everything while it is still light." And so they returned to the dining room and did as before. When all was complete according to the order of the day, everyone hurried to evening prayers. The abbot began to chant the verse:

"God, come to my aid."[29]

Then together they honored the Trinity and so began to chant this verse, singing:

> *"We have acted unjustly, we have committed inequity. You, Lord, who are a faithful father, spare us. In peace I will take my sleep and rest, since you, Lord, alone have given me hope."*[30]

After these words they chanted the holy service of that hour.

When they had finished the order of songs, all the brothers went out from that place to their own cells, taking their guests with them. The abbot, however, remained in the church with holy Brendan, awaiting the coming of the light. Holy Brendan asked the holy father about their silence and ways, wondering how it was possible for human flesh to endure such a life.

The abbot responded with great reverence and humility:

> "Father, I confess this before my Christ. We came to this island eighty years ago. We do not use human voice except when we sing the praises of God. Among the twenty-four of us we do not speak unless a signal is given by a finger or eye, even then only by the elders. Since we came to this place, none of us has suffered any disease of the flesh or from the spirits who wander among the human race.

Then holy Brendan asked, "Is it permitted for us to stay here or not?" And the abbot said:

> "It is not permitted, for it is not the will of God. Why do you ask me this, Father? Didn't God reveal to you what you had to do before you came to us? You must return to your own place with fourteen of your brothers. There God has prepared your burial place. Of the two other brothers, one will stay on the Island of the Anchorites. The other will be condemned to a most shameful death in hell."

While they were discussing these matters, suddenly a fiery arrow came through the window and lit all the lamps placed in front of the altar. The arrow then reversed course and went back out the window. Nonetheless the precious light remained in the lamps. Again blessed Brendan questioned the abbot, "Who extinguishes the lights in the morning?"

And the holy father answered him:

> *"Come and see this miracle yourself. Look at how the wicks burn in the middle of the lamps. Still, they are not diminished nor do they burn down. And no ash remains in the morning, for the light is spiritual."*

Holy Brendan asked, "How can an incorporeal light burn physically in a material creation?"

The old man answered:

> *"Haven't you read of the burning bush on Mount Sinai? The bush itself was untouched by the fire."*[31]

The two men remained at their vigil through the night until morning, when holy Brendan asked permission to begin their journey again. The old man replied:

> *"No, Father. You must celebrate Christmas with us first until the eighth day after Epiphany."*[32]

And so the holy father remained on that island with his monks and the twenty-four brothers who are known as the Community of Ailbe.

THE WELL OF SLEEP

When the feast days were finished and the brothers had accepted provisions and blessings from the holy men, blessed Brendan and his followers unfurled the sails and set out with their little boat into the ocean as quickly as possible. By sail or by rowing the boat traveled here and there until the beginning of Lent.

One day the brothers saw an island not far away. When they saw this, they began to row with all their might toward it since their supplies had run out three days earlier and they were very hungry and thirsty. When the holy father had blessed the landing place and everyone had gotten out of the boat, they found a spring of wondrously clear water there surrounded by all kinds of edible plants and roots, along with many kinds of fish swimming from the spring down a stream to the sea.

Holy Brendan said to his brothers:

> *"God gave to you this reward for your labors. Catch enough fish for our supper and roast them on a fire. Collect also the vegetables and roots which God has prepared for his servants."*

And they did so. But when they had drawn out water for drinking, the man of God said to them, "Brothers, take care that you don't drink too deeply from these waters lest they weigh heavily on your bodies."

The monks heeded the warning of the man of God differently. Some drank a single cup, others two, and still others three. The latter fell into a deep sleep for three days and nights. Those who drank two cups slept two days and nights. And those who drank only one cup slept for just a single day and night. Meanwhile the holy father prayed for them all without ceasing, since because of their foolishness a great danger had befallen them.

When those who had slept for three days at last woke up, the holy father said to his companions:

> "Brothers, let us flee this death before something worse happens to us. The Lord gave us sustenance, but you have made it into a source of harm. Let us leave this island and take enough fish with us to feed us every third day until Maundy Thursday. Also take enough water so that each brother may drink one cup each day. The same also for the roots."

They loaded the boat with all the man of God had ordered, then hoisted the sails and set out into the ocean toward the north.

THE COAGULATED SEA

After three days and three nights the wind ceased and the ocean became so still it was as if it had turned solid. The holy father said:

> *"Draw your oars into the ship and let down the sails.*
> *Wherever God as our guide wishes to lead us, let it be so."*

The boat was therefore carried in a circle for twenty days. After this God again raised a favorable wind for them blowing from the west to the east. So then they raised the sails and began to row. They always ate every third day.

FAMILIAR PLACES

One day an island appeared to them far away that looked like a cloud. Holy Brendan said, "My sons, do you recognize that island?"

And they answered, "Not at all."

But he said:

> *"I recognize it. That is the island where last year we spent*
> *Maundy Thursday. It is where our good steward lives."*

Then the brothers began to row swiftly with joy, as fast as their strength was able to carry them. But when the man of God saw this he said:

> *"Children, do not wear out your limbs in vain. Don't you*
> *know that God almighty is our pilot and the captain of*
> *our little boat? Leave it all to him, for he directs our*
> *journey as he wishes."*

When they came near to the shore of that island, the steward came to them in a small boat and led them to the landing spot they had used the year before. He praised God and kissed the feet of them all, starting with the holy father all the way through the youngest of them, singing:

> *"God is wonderful in his holy people. The God of Israel himself will give strength and courage to his people. Blessed be God."*

When the verse was over and everyone had gotten out of the boat, the steward pitched a tent and made ready a bath—for it was Maundy Thursday—and he clothed all the brothers in new garments and served them for three days. The brothers celebrated the Passion of the Lord there with great care until Holy Saturday.

With the services of that day finished, the holy victims offered in spiritual sacrifice to God, and the dinner eaten, the steward said to holy Brendan and those with him:

> *"Go and get into your boat so that you may spend the night of the resurrection of the Lord where you did last year. Then you may celebrate the day of Easter Sunday itself in the same way until noon. Afterward sail to the island which is called the Paradise of Birds, where you were last year from Easter to the eighth day of Pentecost. Take with you all the food and drink you need. I will come to you there the next Sunday."*

And so they did. The steward loaded the boat with bread and meat and other good foods, as much as it could carry. When holy Brendan had given his blessing, he went into the boat and they immediately set out toward the other island.

When they came near to the place where they would land, they saw there the pot they had left behind the previous year. Then holy Brendan climbed out of the boat with his brothers and began to sing the hymn of the three children through to the end. When this was done, the man of God warned his brothers, saying:

> *"O my sons, watch and pray, so that you not be led into temptation. Reflect on how God has subdued the wild beast beneath us to our benefit."*

The brothers therefore prayed throughout the island until morning prayers. Then each of the priests offered masses to God until midmorning. Blessed Brendan then sacrificed the spotless lamb to God and said to the brothers:

> *"Here last year I celebrated the resurrection of the Lord. I wish to do the same this year."*

After that they set out for the island of birds.

As they were approaching the landing place of that island, all the birds began to sing as if with one voice, saying, "Salvation belongs to our God who sits upon the throne and to the lamb."[33]

And again:

> "The Lord God has given us light.[34] Appoint a holy day
> with boughs to the horn of the altar."

Thus for a long time they sang and beat their wings, until half an hour had passed and the holy father with his holy community and all their goods were removed from the boat and placed into their tent.

After he had celebrated the feast of Easter there with his community, the steward again came to them, just as he had said he would, on Sunday eight days after Easter. He brought with him all the food needed for sustaining human life.

When they sat down at the table, suddenly the same bird as before sat down on the prow of the little boat with its wings stretched out, making a noise like the sound of a great organ. The man of God then realized that it wanted to say something to him. The bird then said:

> "God has ordained four places for you to land over the
> next four years until you finish your seven-year voyage.
> Maundy Thursday you will spend each year with your
> steward, then you will celebrate Easter on the back of the
> whale. The Easter feast until the eighth day after Pente-
> cost you will spend with us. Then every Christmas you
> will be with the community of Ailbe. When seven years
> have passed full of great and diverse trials, you will at
> last find the Land Promised to the Saints which you seek.

You will live there forty days, after which God will lead
you back to the land of your birth."

When the holy father heard this, he prostrated himself on the
ground with his brothers, giving thanks and praise to his creator.
After the venerable old man had finished, the bird went back to his
own place.

The steward then spoke to them when they had finished eating:

"With the help of God I will return to you with your
provisions on the day of the coming of the Holy Spirit to
the apostles."

When he had accepted the blessing of the holy father and all
those with him, he returned to his own place. The venerable father
then remained there the appointed number of days. After the days
of the feast were complete, holy Brendan ordered his brothers to
prepare to sail and to fill the jars from the well. They carried the
boat to the sea just as the steward arrived in his own boat full of
food for the brothers. He put all the provisions in the little boat of
the holy man, then kissed them all and returned to his own home.

A BATTLE OF BEASTS

The venerable father with his companions sailed out into the
ocean and the boat was carried along for forty days. One day there

appeared to them an enormous beast following them at a distance. It spouted foam from its nostrils and cut through the waves with great speed as if it was about to devour them. When the brothers saw it, they cried out to the Lord, saying, "Deliver us, Lord, so that beast does not eat us!"

But holy Brendan comforted them, saying:

> *"Do not be afraid, you men of little faith.*[35] *God, who is always our defender, will save us from the mouth of that beast and from other dangers."*

But as the monster drew near to them, it drove before it waves of amazing height up to the boat so that the brothers grew more and more afraid. Then the venerable old man lifted up his hands to the sky and said:

> *"Lord, deliver your servants, just as you delivered David from the hands of the giant Goliath.*[36] *Lord, deliver us, just as you delivered Jonah from the belly of the great whale."*

After they had made these three pleas, suddenly another huge creature passed by them coming from the west to attack the previous beast. He immediately attacked the first creature with fire shooting from his mouth. Then the old man said to the brothers:

> *"Behold, my sons, the great work of our redeemer. See the
> obedience of beasts to their creator. Wait for the outcome
> of this affair. This battle will bring no evil to us, for it will
> show the glory of God."*

When he had said this, the wretched monster that had pursued
the community of Christ was cut into three pieces before their
faces, then the victorious creature turned back and returned from
where it had come.

On another day they saw a large island far off and covered with
trees. When they had drawn near to the shore and climbed out of
the boat, they saw the rear part of the beast that had been killed.
Holy Brendan said:

> *"Behold the creature that wished to devour you. Now you will
> devour it. You will wait a long time on this island. Therefore
> lift up the boat out of the water high onto the land and look
> for a place in the woods where you can pitch your tent."*

The holy father himself selected a place for them to stay.

When they had followed the orders of the man of God and
brought all their equipment into the tent, holy Brendan said to his
brothers:

> *"Take the meat you need from that creature, enough for
> three months. For tonight its body will be devoured by beasts."*

So they carried meat away until evening, as much as they needed, obeying the orders of the holy father. But when this was finished, they said, "Father, how can we live here without water?"

And he said to them:

> *"Is it more difficult for God to provide water for you than food? Go therefore to the southern shore of this island. There you will find a very pure well along with many plants to eat and root vegetables. Bring back to me an appropriate supply."*

And they found everything there just as the man of God had said. Holy Brendan remained on that island for three months, for there was a terrible storm on the sea with strong winds along with rain and hail.

The brothers went to see if what the man of God had said about the beast was true. When they came to the place where the carcass had lain earlier, they saw nothing there except bones. They returned to the man of God, saying, "Father, it happened just like you said."

And he said to them:

> *"My sons, I know that you wanted to test me to see if what I said was true or not. Now I'll give you another sign: a large piece of that same fish will wash up there tonight and tomorrow you shall eat of it."*

The following day the brothers went out to the same spot and found that what the man of God had said was true. They carried back as much meat as they were able. The venerable father said to them:

> *"Preserve this meat carefully with salt, for you are going to need it. The Lord will make the weather calm today and tomorrow and the next day so that the swell of the sea and waves will cease. After that you will leave this place."*

When these days had passed, holy Brendan ordered his brothers to load up the boat and to fill the skins and other vessels. He also ordered them to collect herbs and root vegetables for his own use, since he had not eaten anything that had once held the breath of life since he became a priest. When everything was loaded into the boat, they raised the sails and set off to the north.

THE ISLAND OF STRONG MEN

One day they saw an island far from them. Holy Brendan said, "Do you see that island?"

And they said, "We see it."

He said to them:

> *"Three groups are on that island: one of boys, one of young men, and one of elders. One of your brothers will remain there."*

The brothers all asked him which of them it would be. When they kept asking and he saw that they were sad, he said, "That is the brother who will remain there."

The brother he pointed out was one of the three who had come to holy Brendan from the monastery. He had spoken of him to the brothers earlier when they came to the boat in their own country.

They drew near to the island until the boat reached the shore. That island was exceedingly flat, so much that it seemed level with the sea. It had no trees or anything that might be moved by the wind. It was very spacious and covered with white and purple fruit. The brothers saw three groups there, just as the man of God had predicted. The space between the groups was about the distance one might throw a stone from a sling. The groups were always moving about from here to there until one group stopped in a place and began to sing:

> *"The saints will go from strength to strength and will see*
> *the God of gods in Zion."* [37]

When one group had finished the verse, another group stood and began to sing that song so that there was no pause. The first group made up of boys was clothed in shining white, while the second wore blue garments and the third purple.

It was ten o'clock when the boat reached the landing place on the shore. When noon came all the groups began to sing together, "May God have mercy on us," [38] until the end, and "God, to my help." [39]

Likewise the third psalm, "I believed,"[40] and the prayer as above.

And again at three o'clock they sang another three psalms: "From the depths,"[41] and "Behold, how good,"[42] and "Praise the Lord, O Jerusalem."[43]

At evening prayers they sang "A hymn is due to you, O God, in Zion,"[44] and "Bless the Lord, my soul,"[45] and "Lord, my God," and the third psalm, "Praise, children, the Lord,"[46] and the fifteen gradual psalms[47] as they sat down.

When they had finished that song, suddenly a cloud of amazing brightness covered the island and they were no longer able to see what they had seen before because of the thickness of the cloud. But they could still hear the voices of those singing without interruption until the early morning prayers. Then the groups began to sing again, chanting "Praise the Lord from the heavens,"[48] then "Sing to the Lord,"[49] and finally "Praise the Lord in his holy places."[50] After this they sang twelve psalms in the order of the psalm book.

When day brightened the sky, the cloud lifted from the island and immediately they began to sing three psalms: "Have mercy on me, God,"[51] and "God, my God, from dawn I will seek you,"[52] and "Lord, my refuge."[53]

At midmorning prayers they sang another three: "All people,"[54] and "God, in your name,"[55] and a third, "I have loved because,"[56] with the Alleluia.

Then they offered up the spotless lamb and everyone came to communion, singing:

> *"This sacred body of the Lord and blood of the savior re-*
> *ceive for eternal life."*

When the service was over, two from the group of young men
brought a basket full of purple fruit and placed it in the boat, saying:

> *"Receive this fruit of the Island of Strong Men. Return*
> *now our brother to us and depart in peace."*

Then holy Brendan called this brother and said to him:

> *"Kiss your brothers and go with them who call you.*
> *Blessed was the hour when your mother conceived you*
> *since you have earned the right to live with such a*
> *community."*

After he had kissed everyone including the holy father, holy Brendan said to him:

> *"Son, remember how many good things God has done for*
> *you in this world. Go now and pray for us."*

The brother immediately followed the two young men back to
their school.

Then the venerable father with his companions set sail. When
noon came, he ordered his brothers to refresh their bodies with
the fruit of the Island of Strong Men. After he said this, the man of

God took one of the fruit from them. When he saw the size of the fruit and how full of juice it was, he was amazed and said, "Never have I seen or read about fruit of such a size." All the pieces of fruit were of equal size and shaped like a large ball. Then the man of God called for a vessel to be brought to him. He squeezed one of the fruit and got a pound of juice from it, which the holy father divided into twelve portions. He gave each man a single portion. Thus for twelve days they lived on a single fruit each day, keeping always in their mouths the taste of honey.

THE ISLAND OF GRAPES

After a few days had passed, the holy father ordered a fast of three days. When these three days were done, suddenly an enormous bird flew near the boat. It was carrying a branch from an unknown tree with a large cluster of amazingly red grapes at the end, which the bird dropped from its mouth into the lap of the holy man. Then holy Brendan called his brothers to him and said, "See and take the reward that God has sent to you."

The grapes were the size of apples. The man of God divided them and gave each brother a single grape so that they had enough food for twelve days.

Again the man of God ordered a fast as before for his brothers. Then after three days they saw an island not far away. The whole island was incredibly fertile and covered with thick trees bearing the same kind of grapes as before, so that the trees were all bent down to the ground with the same sort of fruit of the same color. No tree was without grapes and there was no other kind of tree on that island.

The brothers soon arrived at a landing place. The man of God got out of the boat and began to walk around the island. It had the smell of a home full of pomegranates. The brothers meanwhile waiting in the boat for the man of God to return to them as the wind blew the sweetest of aromas to them, tempting them to break their fast.

The venerable father discovered six flowing springs with green plants and many kinds of roots. When he had returned to the boat carrying with him the first fruits of the island, he said to the brothers:

> "Come out from the ship and pitch your tent. Refresh yourselves with the best fruits of this land which the Lord has given to you."

And so for forty days they renewed themselves with the grapes, plants, and roots from the springs. Then after that time they climbed back into the boat carrying with them as much of the fruit as the little craft could bear.

THE GRIFFIN

After they had set out, they raised the sail and let the boat go as the wind blew it. While they were sailing, a bird appeared to them called a griffin,[57] far away but flying toward them. When the brothers saw this they said to the holy father, "That beast is coming to eat us!" But the man of God replied, "Do not be afraid. God is our helper who will defend us this time as well."

Just as the monster was stretching out its claws to seize the servants of God, suddenly the same bird, which had earlier brought them the branch with fruit, attacked the griffin. The beast tried to devour that bird, but it defended itself and even tore the eyes out of the griffin. The monster then flew high into the sky so that the brothers could barely see it. But the bird pursued the griffin until it killed it and the body of the beast fell into the sea next to the boat in front of the brothers. The bird then returned to its home.

RETURN TO THE COMMUNITY OF AILBE

After a few days holy Brendan and his fellow sailors saw again the Island of the Community of Ailbe. There he celebrated Christmas with his brothers. When the feast days were finished, the venerable father accepted the blessing of the abbot and his monks, then sailed around the ocean for a long time—except for the feasts previously mentioned, Easter and Christmas. At those times he stayed at the appointed places.

THE CLEAR SEA

One day when holy Brendan was celebrating the feast of Saint Peter the Apostle[58] on the boat, they came upon a part of the sea so clear that they were able to see everything below them. When they looked into the deep they saw many kinds of creatures lying on the seabed. The water was so clear that it seemed they would be able to touch them. The creatures were like herds lying in a pasture. There were so many of them that they looked like a city of circles with their heads touching their tails.

The brothers asked the venerable father to celebrate Mass in silence so that the beasts might not hear him and rise up to chase them. But the holy father laughed and said to them:

> *"I marvel at your foolishness. Why are you afraid of these beasts but not that great monarch of the sea who devours all creatures? Many times you have sat on his back singing psalms. You even gathered sticks on him and kindled a fire to cook meat. So why are you afraid of these? Don't you know that our Lord Jesus Christ is God of all beasts and can tame every animal?"*

When he had said this, he began to sing as loudly as he could. All the brothers began to watch the animals beneath them with great care. As soon as the beasts heard the voice of the singer, they rose up from the floor of the sea and began to swim in a circle around the boat so that the brothers were not able to see anything anywhere but swimming creatures. Nonetheless they did not come near the boat but swam at a distance here and there until the man of God finished singing the Mass. Then they departed, all swimming away from the servants of God to different parts of the ocean. Even with a favorable wind on the billowing sails, it took holy Brendan eight days to sail across that clear sea.

THE CRYSTAL COLUMN

On a certain day when they had finished celebrating their masses, a column appeared in the sea before them which did not seem far away. Nonetheless, it took them three days to draw near. When the man of God came close to it, he looked up to its summit, but could scarcely see the top because of its height. It was higher than the sky. The column was surrounded by a wide-meshed net, so wide that a boat could sail through one of the openings. They could not tell what material the net was made from. It had the color of silver, but seemed harder than marble. The column itself was of the clearest crystal.[59]

Holy Brendan said to his brothers:

> *"Draw in the oars and take down the mast and sails. The rest of you take hold of the mesh of the net."*

The net was so wide that it extended a mile out from the column and stretched the same distance down into the sea.

When the brothers had finished their tasks, the man of God said to them, "Draw the boat in through one of the openings so that we might see the great works of our creator."

They came inside the net and looked this way and that. The sea there appeared to them as clear as glass so that they could gaze on everything beneath them. They were able to look down to the base of the column and at the end of the net lying on the seafloor. The light of the sun was not any less below them than it was above.

Then holy Brendan measured the four sides of one of the openings of the net. It was four cubits on each side. For that whole day they sailed next to one side of the column. Even in the shadow it cast they were able to feel the heat of the sun. They did this until midafternoon, with the man of God measuring one side. Each of the four sides was one thousand four hundred cubits long. Thus for four days the venerable father sailed around the four corners of that column measuring it.

On the fourth day they discovered a chalice made from the same material as the net and a paten the same color as the column, both lying inside a window on the southern side of the column. Holy Brendan immediately took these vessels, saying:

> *"Our Lord Jesus Christ has revealed to us this miracle so that we might show these gifts to many and they might believe me."*

Immediately the man of God ordered the brothers to celebrate the divine office and afterward to refresh their bodies, for they had not had anything to eat or drink while they sailed around the column.

When that night had passed, the brothers began to sail north. When they had come to a certain opening in the net, some raised the mast and sails as others held open the mesh of the net while the boat was prepared. When everything was ready, a favorable wind began to rise behind them so that they needed to do nothing except hold the ropes and rudder. Thus for eight days the little boat was carried toward the north.

THE ISLAND OF SMITHS

After eight days, they saw an island not far away. It was rough, rocky, and full of slag, with no trees or plants. It was full of forges used by smiths. The venerable father said to his brothers:

> *"Truly, brothers, I am troubled by this island and do not wish to land there or even draw near, though that is where the wind is blowing us."*

As they were sailing close to the island, about as far as one might throw a stone, they heard the sound of a bellows blowing as if it were thunder and the pounding of a hammer on iron and anvils. When he heard this, the venerable father armed himself by making the sign of the cross in four directions, saying, "Lord Jesus Christ, deliver us from this island."

When the man of God finished speaking, suddenly one of the inhabitants of that island came out of his hut to do something. He was quite hairy and full of fire and shadow. When he saw the brothers of Christ sailing near the island, he ran back into his workshop. The man of God then armed himself and said to the brothers:

> "My sons, raise the sail higher and row as fast as you can.
> We must flee this island."

Even while he was speaking, the barbaric creature ran to the shore near to them carrying tongs in which he held an immense, burning lump of fiery slag. He immediately threw the lump at the brothers of Christ, but it did not harm them, for it passed more than six hundred feet over their heads. At the spot where it fell into the water, the sea began to boil like an underwater volcano. The smoke rose up from the water like a furnace of fire.

When the man of God had sailed about a mile away from where the lump had fallen, all the creatures who lived on that island ran to the shore, each carrying his own lump of burning slag. They began to throw their lumps at the brothers of Christ, one lump landing beyond the other. They kept running back into their workshops to stoke their forges, so that it seemed as if the whole island were on fire like one giant furnace. The sea itself boiled as if it were a giant pot of cooking meat set over a roaring fire. All that day the brothers heard horrible cries from that island. Even when they could no longer see the place, they could still hear the cries of the creatures in their ears and smell the harsh odor of fire in their noses.

At last the holy father comforted the monks, saying:

> *"O soldiers of Christ, be strong with your well-founded faith and spiritual weapons, for we are at the borders of hell. Be watchful, therefore, and fight bravely."*

THE FIERY MOUNTAIN

On another day a high mountain appeared to them close by in the north seeming to be covered with clouds of great smoke at its summit. A sudden wind sprang up and drove them to the shore of that island until the boat came to rest a short distance from land. The cliff there was so high that they were scarcely able to see the summit. The slope was the color of coal and as steep as a wall.

One of the brothers, the last of the three who had followed holy Brendan from his monastery, jumped out of the boat and began to walk up to the foot of the cliff. He shouted, saying:

> *"Woe to me, father. I am taken from you and do not have the power to return."*

The brothers immediately turned the boat away from the island and cried out to the Lord, saying:

> *"Have mercy on us, Lord. Have mercy on us."*

The venerable father and his companions saw that unlucky man led away to torment by a multitude of demons and watched as he was set on fire in the midst of them. Holy Brendan said to him:

> *"Woe to you, my son, for you have received in this life the punishment you deserved."*

Soon a favorable wind arose and carried them away to the south. When they looked back at the island from far away, they saw the mountain cleared of smoke but shooting forth flames into the air and breathing them back into itself. The whole mountain down to the sea seemed as if it were a single pyre.

JUDAS

When holy Brendan had sailed south for seven days, there appeared to the brothers in the sea a shape that looked like a man sitting on a rock. There was a cloth hanging about the length of a cloak in front of it between two iron forks. The figure was buffeted by the waves just like a little boat caught in a storm. Some of the brothers said that it was a bird, while others thought it was a boat. When the man of God heard them saying such things among themselves, he said, "Stop arguing. Steer the boat toward it."

As the man of God approached that place, the waves surrounded it in what seemed like a solid circle. They then discovered it was a man shaggy and disfigured sitting there on a rock. From every side the waves pounded him, striking even the top of his head. When the waves receded, the rock appeared bare with the unfortunate man sitting there. The cloth that was hanging in front of him would sometimes blow away from him and other times strike him on the eyes and forehead.

Blessed Brendan began to ask him who he was and for what sin he had been sent there or what he had done to deserve such a penance. The man replied:

> "I am Judas,[60] the most unfortunate and the greatest of traitors. I am not here because of my own merit but because of the unspeakable mercy of Jesus Christ. This is not a place of punishment but of rest given by the savior in honor of his resurrection."

For that day was Sunday.

> "It seems to me, as I sit here, that I am in the most delightful paradise—for I greatly fear the place I will be this evening. There I burn like molten lead in a crucible day and night in the middle of that mountain you saw. Leviathan lives there with his companions. I was there when he devoured your brother. Hell was so delighted that it sent forth towering flames as it always does when it consumes a wicked

soul. I am allowed to rest here every Sunday from one evening prayer to the next. I am also here from Christmas to
Epiphany, from Easter to Pentecost, and on the feasts of the
purification and assumption of the Mother of God. During
the rest of the year I am tortured in the depths of hell with
Herod,[61] Pilate,[62] Annas,[63] and Caiaphas.[64] I therefore beg
of you by the savior of the world to please intercede for me
with the Lord Jesus Christ that I may stay here until the
rising of the sun tomorrow, so that the demons might not
drag me off to torment at your arrival and subject me to
that hideous fate I purchased at so terrible a price."

And holy Brendan said to him:

"Let the will of the Lord be done. You will not be consumed
by demons from this night until the morning."

Then the man of God questioned him, saying, "What is the meaning of this cloth?"
    And he answered:

"I gave this cloth to a leper when I was the chamberlain
of the Lord. But it was not mine to give, for it belonged to
the Lord and his brothers. Now it brings me no comfort,
but rather harm. As for the iron forks on which the cloth
hangs, I gave those to the priests of the temple for holding
up cooking pots. The rock on which I sit, before I was a

*disciple of the Lord I placed that in a ditch across a
public road to support the feet of those passing by."*

When the evening hour darkened the sky, suddenly a multitude
of countless demons began to circle the face of the heavens, shouting and saying:

*"Go away from us, man of God, for we cannot come near
our companion until you leave him. Nor do we dare to
look on the face of our prince until we return his friend
to him. You are keeping us from our food. Do not protect
him this night."*

The man of God said to them:

*"It is not I who defend him, but the Lord Jesus Christ has
allowed him to remain here tonight until the morning."*

Then the demons said:

*"How can you invoke the name of the Lord for this man
when he is the very one who betrayed him?"*

The man of God said to them, "I command you in the name of our
Lord Jesus Christ that you do nothing to this man until morning."

When the night had passed and dawn was coming, the man of
God began to prepare to set out again on his journey. Behold then

a multitude of demons appeared over the face of the sea, crying out in terrifying voices and saying:

> *"O man of God, cursed is your coming and going, for last*
> *night our prince scourged us with horrible whips because*
> *we did not bring his wicked captive to him."*

The man of God said to them:

> *"Your curses do not fall on us, but rather yourselves. The*
> *one you curse is blessed, just as the one you bless is cursed."*

The demons answered him, "Unfortunate Judas will suffer double for the next six days since you protected him this night."

The venerable father then said, "You do not have that power, nor does your prince. God will have that power." And he added:

> *"I command you and your prince in the name of the Lord*
> *Jesus Christ not to torture him more than before."*

They responded, "Are you the Lord of all that we should obey your words?"

And the man of God said to them:

> *"I am his servant and whatever I order is in his name. I*
> *have authority over those things he has granted me."*

The demons followed the boat until the brothers were no longer able to see Judas. Then the demons turned back and raised that most unfortunate soul into their embrace with great force and screaming.

PAUL THE HERMIT

Holy Brendan and his fellow soldiers sailed on to the south, glorifying God in all things. On the third day a certain small island appeared to them far away in the south. When the brothers began to row faster and had drawn near to that island, holy Brendan said to them:

> "Men, brothers, do not wear out your bodies. You have worked hard enough. When this Easter soon approaches, it will have been seven years since we set out from our homeland. Now you are about to meet Paul the spiritual hermit who has lived on this island without bodily food for sixty years. For thirty years before that he received his food from an animal."

But when they drew near to the shore, they were not able to find a place to land, for the cliffs around that island were high. The island was small and circular, about six hundred feet across. There was hardly any soil on it, only bare rock that looked like flint. It was as long as it was broad and just as high. When they had circled the whole island, at last they found a landing place so narrow they could barely force the bow of the boat into it. The narrowness of

the place made it very difficult to climb out of the boat. Then holy
Brendan said to his brothers:

> *"Wait here until I return to you. You are not allowed to*
> *come onto the island without the permission of the man*
> *of God who lives in this place."*

When the venerable father came to the top of that island, he saw
two caves on the eastern side with their mouths facing each other. A
small spring was there as well, round like a plate, from which water
flowed from the rock to the mouth of the cave where the soldier of
Christ lived. When the spring overflowed, the rock immediately ab-
sorbed it. Thus as holy Brendan came near to the mouth of one cave,
an old man came out from the other to meet him, saying, "Behold,
how good and joyful it is when brothers live together."[65]

After he said this, he told holy Brendan to call all the brothers
from the boat. As they kissed him and sat down, he called each of
them by name. The brothers were amazed and marveled not only
at his power of prophesy but at the way he was dressed. His whole
body from head to foot was covered with his own hair and beard.
This was as white as snow because of his extreme age. Only his
face and eyes were visible. He was wearing nothing except the hair
that grew from his own body. When holy Brendan saw this, he was
sorrowful in his heart, saying:

> *"Woe is me, for I wear the clothing of a monk and have*
> *many under my authority who are members of my order.*

> *But I see sitting before me a man already in that angelic*
> *state untouched by the vices of the body."*

The man of God then spoke to holy Brendan.

> *"O venerable father, God has shown you so many and such*
> *great miracles hidden even from the holy fathers of old.*
> *You say in your heart that you are not worthy to wear the*
> *clothing of a monk, but you are greater than a monk. A*
> *monk labors by the work of his hands to feed and clothe*
> *himself, but God himself in his mysterious ways has fed*
> *and clothed you and your companions for seven years. But*
> *I sit here on this rock like a bird, naked except for my*
> *hair."*

Then holy Brendan questioned him about his coming to that
place and his origin and how long he had lived such a life. The man
answered him:

> *"I was raised in the monastery of holy Patrick for fifty*
> *years where I took care of the cemetery of the brothers. One*
> *day when my supervisor had shown me a place to bury a*
> *brother who had died, an old and unknown man appeared*
> *to me and said, 'Brother, do not make a grave there, for it*
> *is the resting place of another.' And I said to him, 'Father,*
> *who are you?' And he said, 'Don't you recognize me? Aren't*
> *I your own abbot?' And I said to him, 'Are you holy Patrick,*

my abbot?' And he said, 'I am. I left this life yesterday. That is the place for my own tomb. Here make the grave of our brother and tell no one what I said to you. Tomorrow go down to the shore of the sea and you will find a little boat there. Get into that boat and it will take you to a place where you will wait until the day of your death.'

The following morning I obeyed the command of the holy father and went down to the shore and found the boat which he had said would be waiting for me. I got into the boat and sailed for three days and three nights. When this time had passed, I let the boat take me wherever it wanted. After seven days this rocky island appeared to me. I climbed out onto it immediately, then pushed the boat away with my foot so that it might go back to the place from where it came. I saw it speed away over the waves like a plow cutting through a field so that it returned to its home. But I stayed here. In the middle of the afternoon an otter brought me a meal from the sea, a fish he was carrying in his mouth, and a bundle of wood to make a fire carried between his front paws. He came walking on his two hind legs. When he had placed before me the fish and firewood, he returned from where he had come. I took some iron and struck it on flint to make a fire with the wood and prepared a meal from the fish. So for thirty years the same servant always brought me the same meal, a fish every third day. I ate a third part of the fish each day. By the grace of God I was not thirsty, but on

Sundays a little trickle of water would come from that rock. From this I could fill my little container and wash my hands. After thirty years I found these two caves and this spring. From this I have lived for sixty years without any other nourishment, only the water from this spring. I have lived ninety years on this island. Thirty years I lived on fish and sixty years on the nourishment of this spring. For fifty years before that I lived in my native land. Thus the years of my life are one hundred and forty. Here I will stay, as was told to me, awaiting in the flesh the day of my judgment. Go, therefore, to your homeland and take with you vessels filled from this fountain. This will be necessary for you because a journey of forty days lies before you until Holy Saturday. You will celebrate Holy Saturday and Easter and the holy days of Easter where you have celebrated them for the last six years. After that you will accept the blessings of your steward, then you will arrive at the Land Promised to the Saints. There you will remain forty days, after which the God of your fathers will bring you safe and unharmed to the land of your birth."

FAMILIAR ISLANDS

Holy Brendan and his brothers accepted the blessing of the man of God, then sailed south for the forty days of Lent. The little boat was carried here and there on the sea. The only food they had was the water they had taken from the island of the man of God. They drank this every third day and all remained joyful without hunger or thirst.

Then, as the man of God had said, they came to the island of the steward on Holy Saturday. When they arrived at the landing place, that man ran up to them with great joy and helped each of them out of the boat with his arms. When the divine offices of the holy day were finished, he placed a meal before them. That evening they climbed back into the boat and the steward came with them.

After sailing, they found Jasconius in his usual place. There they sang praise to God all night and celebrated Mass in the morning. But when Mass was finished, the creature began to go his own way. All the brothers with holy Brendan began to cry out to the Lord, saying:

> *"Hear us, God, our salvation, the hope of all in the boundaries of the earth and on the deep sea."*[66]

Holy Brendan comforted his brothers, saying, "Do not be afraid. No evil will befall you. Help for our journey is at hand."

The creature kept a straight course to the Island of the Birds. There they stayed until the eighth day of Pentecost.

When the feast days were complete, the steward who was with them said to holy Brendan:

> *"Go up into your little boat and fill your water skins from that fountain. I will now be your companion and guide*

*on this journey, for without me you would not be able to
find the Land Promised to the Saints."*

As they went up into the boat, all the birds which were on the island began to sing as if with one voice, "May God our salvation make your journey prosperous."

THE LAND PROMISED TO THE SAINTS

Holy Brendan and those with him sailed back to the island of the steward with him traveling with them and there took on supplies for forty days. Then they sailed in their boat for forty days to the east. The steward sat at the front of the boat and guided their journey. When forty days had passed and evening had come, a great fog began to surround them so that they were scarcely able to see each other. The steward then said to holy Brendan, "Do you know what fog this is?"

And holy Brendan said, "What is it?"

Then the steward said, "This fog surrounds that island you have been seeking for seven years."

After about an hour a great light shone all around them and the boat reached the shore.

When they had left the boat, they saw a wide land full of fruit-bearing trees just as if it were autumn. But after they had walked around on the island, night had still not come upon them. They took as much fruit as they wanted and drank from the springs. Thus for forty days they explored the island but were not able to find the end of it.

One day they discovered a great river flowing through the middle of the island. Then holy Brendan said to his brothers:

> *"We are not able to cross that river. We are not able to*
> *know how large this island is."*

While they were pondering these things among themselves, suddenly a young man appeared to them. He kissed each of them with great joy and called them all by name. Then he said to them:

> *"Blessed are those who live in your home. They will praise*
> *you from age to age."*[67]

When he had said this, he spoke to holy Brendan:

> *"Behold, this is the land which you have sought for so long.*
> *You were not able to find it immediately because God*
> *wanted to show you the many secret wonders of the great*
> *ocean. Now return to the land of your birth, carrying with*
> *you the fruit of this island and as many stones from here*
> *as your boat will bear. The day of your pilgrimage draws*
> *near when you will sleep with your fathers. After many*
> *cycles of time this land will become known to your succes-*
> *sors, when a time of persecution of Christians comes. That*
> *river you saw divides this island. Even as it appears to you*

> *now full of ripe fruit, so will this island be for all time,*
> *without darkness. For Christ is the light of this place."*

They collected the fruit of the island and all kinds of stones. Then with the blessing of the steward and the young man, holy Brendan and his brothers climbed into their little boat and began to sail away through the fog. When they had passed through it, they found the Island of Delight. There for three days they enjoyed hospitality. Then with blessings received, holy Brendan sailed straight back to his own land.

RETURNING HOME

The brothers there welcomed him with great joy and glorified God, who had not wished them to be deprived of the loving father from whom they had so long been separated like orphans. Then the blessed man praised their love and told them everything that had happened to him on his journey and the marvelous wonders God had shown them on their voyage.

Finally he told them of his soon-approaching death as foretold by the young man on the Land Promised to the Saints. This event proved to be true, for as soon as he had taken care of all necessary affairs, it was only a short period of time before he died, fortified by the divine sacraments. He passed gloriously from the hands of his disciples to the Lord, to whom is honor and glory from age to age.

Amen. This is the end.

NOTES

SAINT PATRICK'S LETTER TO THE SOLDIERS

1   Patrick writes this letter himself as does the Apostle Paul in sections of his own New Testament letters (Philippians 2.30, Matthew 26.38) to signify special authority.

2   1 Corinthians 16.21, Galatians 6.11, Colossians 4.18, 2 Thessalonians 3.17, Philemon 19.

3   In Patrick's opinion, Coroticus and his men have lost the noble title of "Roman" because of their barbarian actions against fellow Christians.

4   The Picts were inhabitants of northernmost Britain in the lands not conquered by the Romans. The southern Picts were first evangelized by the missionary Nennius, probably in the years just before Patrick's mission to Ireland. *Apostate* is a term normally used to describe someone who has accepted, then rejected, Christianity, though here it is perhaps used of the Picts in a more generalized negative sense.

5   There is an echo here of the parable of the landowner who sends his son to deal with the wicked tenants of his vineyard (Matthew 21.33–41).

6   John 8.34.

7   Ephesians 6.20.

8   Psalm 53.4, Acts 20.29.

9   Psalm 119.126.

10   Acts 13.47.

11   Matthew 16.19.

12   1 Corinthians 5.11.

13   Sirach 34.23–24.

14   Job 20.15–16, 26.

15   Habakkuk 2.6.

16   Matthew 16.26.

17 This passage is not found in scripture, though greed is often condemned (e.g., Luke 12.15).
18 Exodus 20.17, Romans 13.9.
19 Exodus 20.13, Romans 13.9.
20 Not found directly in scripture, though probably based on 1 Peter 4.15.
21 1 John 3.15.
22 1 John 3.14.
23 Acts 20.22.
24 A privileged member of the city council in a Roman town, decurions collected imperial taxes and performed other important public duties in the later Roman Empire. The office was hereditary, so that Patrick would have inherited it from his father.
25 John 4.44.
26 Matthew 12.30.
27 Sirach 34.28.
28 Jeremiah 16.16, Acts 2.17, Joel 2.28–29.
29 Matthew 7.15.
30 Genesis 3.6.
31 The Franks were a Germanic tribe on the middle and lower Rhine who frequently raided and finally settled in Roman Gaul. Augustine condemned the kidnapping of Christians by slave traders and used church funds to ransom them (*Epistle* 10).
32 1 Corinthians 6.15.
33 Romans 1.32.
34 Romans 12.15; 1 Corinthians 12.26.
35 1 Corinthians 4.14–15.
36 Malachi 2.10.
37 Philippians 2.16.
38 Revelation 22.15, 21.4.
39 Malachi 4.2–3.
40 Matthew 8.11–12.
41 Revelation 21.8, 22.15.
42 1 Peter 4.18, Proverbs 11.31.
43 Psalm 68.2–3.
44 Mark 16.16.

SAINT PATRICK'S CONFESSION

1 Although we have no independent contemporary record of Patrick's family, the variant name *Calpurnius* is found in several inscriptions from Roman Britain.

2 Deacons served many practical and liturgical functions in the early church, such as assistance at baptism and the Eucharist, as well as ministering to the needy, though they could not celebrate the Eucharist as priests could.

3 From the Latin *presbyter*, an ordained Christian minister responsible, among his other duties, for teaching, baptizing, and celebrating the Eucharist. Priests were allowed to marry.

4 A town of unknown location, but presumably near the western coast of Britain. The manuscripts preserve the name variously but most often as *Bannavem Taburniae*. Since this makes no sense as either a Roman or a British Celtic name, I have followed the suggested emendation of other scholars (see Rivet and Smith, *Place-Names of Roman Britain,* 511–512).

5 Isaiah 42.25, Leviticus 26.33, Jeremiah 9.16, Ezekiel 4.13, Tobit 13.5.

6 Joel 2.12.

7 Whatever its immediate origins, this informal creed is a profound yet simple expression of Patrick's faith and shows Patrick's theology was very much in line with the orthodox Christianity of his time.

8 John 1.3.

9 Philippians 2.11.

10 Romans 2.6.

11 Titus 3.6.

12 Psalm 50.15.

13 Tobit 12.7.

14 Psalm 5.6.

15 Wisdom of Solomon 1.11.

16 Matthew 12.36.

17 Sirach 4.29.

18 Isaiah 32.4.

19 2 Corinthians 3.2–3.

20 Sirach 7.15.

21 A Roman mile was approximately 4850 feet (1478 meters), somewhat
    less than a modern mile. Thus 200 Roman miles would be roughly 180
    modern miles (290 kilometers). Depending on where Patrick began his
    journey, this means that he traveled almost the entire length of Ireland
    during his escape.

22 This odd phrase (Latin: *sugere mammellas eorum*) seems to indicate a pagan
    ritual of initiation and is attested elsewhere in Irish literature as well as
    in other cultures (see Maier, "*Sugere Mammellas*").

23 This location is unknown, though westernmost Britain is likely. Patrick
    in this passage deliberately parallels his experiences to that of the Israel-
    ites wandering through the desert after they fled from Egypt.

24 These dogs were probably part of the cargo. Large Irish dogs, likely
    wolfhounds, were imported to Rome during the latter days of the Empire
    to be used in public spectacles (Symmachus, *Letter* 2.77).

25 1 Corinthians 10.28.

26 A strange episode drawing on the similarity between the Hebrew prophet
    Elijah (Latin: *Helias*) and the sun god *Helios*. Elijah ascending into heaven
    in his fiery chariot (2 Kings 2.11–12) was a frequent image in early
    Christian iconography, much as Helios in his own chariot was in pagan
    art.

27 Matthew 10.19–20.

28 This episode is similar to God's calling of the prophet Samuel (1 Samuel
    3.1–18).

29 Although he comes from Ireland, Victoricus bears a Roman name. Per-
    haps he was a fellow captive of Patrick or a friend from his youth in
    Britain.

30 This may have been the place of Patrick's captivity. The early Irish writer
    Tírechán places it in modern County Mayo.

31 Possibly a nickname given to Patrick during his captivity by his master or
    fellow slaves because of his frequent prayers.

32 Latin: *nescio, Deus scit*—a frequent expression of Patrick, probably taken
    from 2 Corinthians 12.3.

33 Ephesians 3.16.

34 Romans 8.26.

35 1 John 2.1, Romans 8.27.

36 Zechariah 2.8.
37 Romans 12.1.
38 Jeremiah 16.19.
39 Isaiah 49.6, Acts 13.47.
40 Matthew 8.11.
41 Matthew 4.19.
42 Jeremiah 16.16.
43 Matthew 28.19–20.
44 Mark 16.15–16.
45 Matthew 24.14.
46 Joel 2.28–29, Acts 2.17–18.
47 Hosea 1.10, Romans 9.25–26.
48 Romans 7.24, 2 Peter 1.13.
49 Galatians 1.20.
50 2 Timothy 4.7.
51 Proverbs 10.1.
52 Matthew 18.7, Romans 2.24.
53 1 Samuel 12.3.
54 Psalm 55.22.
55 Matthew 20.22, Mark 10.38.
56 Romans 8.17.

THE FIRST SYNOD OF SAINT PATRICK

1 The death dates of these latter two bishops are listed in the Irish annals as 459 and 468, respectively.
2 Sirach 20.2.
3 A lector was a member of a lower order of the clergy who read or sang the scriptures during the liturgy.
4 A member of the lowest order of the clergy. His responsibilities included opening and closing of the church doors and guarding the building.
5 The tonsure or cutting of hair in a specific fashion was the mark of a clergyman and his dedication to divine service. The Roman tonsure used in

Western Europe involved shaving only the top of the head. The earliest Christian Irish tonsure was a shaving of the front of the head from ear to ear.

6　Latin: *aruspex*; in the Irish context almost certainly a druid.

7　In Roman folklore, a *lamia* was a female monster or witch said to suck the blood of children.

8　From the Latin *striga*, a creature or witch that howled in the night and sucked blood.

9　In traditional Irish law, the groom paid a *coibche* or bride price to a woman's father. If a divorce occurred that was the fault of the woman, the bride price had to be returned to the husband (Kelly, *A Guide to Early Irish Law,* 72–73).

THE HYMN OF SAINT SECUNDINUS

1　Matthew 16.18.
2　Mark 1.17.
3　Exodus 16.
4　Matthew 5.14–16.
5　Matthew 22.1–14.
6　In early Christian literature, the name *Israel* was often interpreted as "seeing God."
7　Matthew 5.13.
8　Mark 4.3–9.
9　The final book of the New Testament, also called *Revelation*.
10　1 Thessalonians 5.17.
11　Matthew 19.28, Luke 22.30.

"SAINT PATRICK'S BREASTPLATE"

1　Loíguire was high king of Ireland in the mid-fifth century according to the Irish Annals. He is featured as a prominent adversary of Patrick in Muirchú's *Life of Saint Patrick*.

2   Tara, in modern County Meath, was the traditional seat of the high kings of Ireland.

3   Patrick's young follower Benignus in Muirchú's *Life of Saint Patrick*.

4   A type of angel particularly devoted to guarding sacred places and objects, as well as to the service of God (e.g., Genesis 3.24, Exodus 25.20, Ezekiel 10).

5   Abraham, Isaac, and Jacob, the three ancestors of the people of Israel.

6   In early Christianity, those who professed a belief in Christ publically in the face of persecution and death.

7   In a late first-century AD inscription from Larzac found in modern France and written in the Gaulish language, the phrase *bnanom bricton* ("the magic of women") is used, words closely related to the Old Irish *brichtu ban* of this passage.

8   In ancient Ireland, smiths were thought to have magical power.

9   The religious leaders of pre-Christian Ireland and elsewhere in the Celtic world.

MUIRCHÚ'S *LIFE OF SAINT PATRICK*

1   Bishop of Sleaty near modern Carlow.

2   Muirchú is deliberately modeling his prologue on that found in the Gospel of Luke (1.1–4).

3   Although Muirchú is using a voyaging metaphor common in early Christian literature, he may also be making a pun on his own Irish name, which means "sea hound."

4   The author of the *Life of Saint Brigid*.

5   This section is badly garbled in the surviving manuscripts. I have included those sections I deemed both relevant and reasonably well attested.

6   A bishop near Navan in County Meath in the generation before Muirchú who collected information on Patrick and perhaps other early Irish saints. His work does not survive.

7   The manuscript is corrupt here.

8   Based on the Old Irish word *cethair* ("four").
9   *Calpornius* in Patrick's *Confession*.
10   See *Bannaventa Berniae* in Patrick's *Confession*.
11   This place is unknown.
12   Exodus 21.2, Deuteronomy 15.12.
13   Psalms 2.11, 55.5.
14   Matthew 22.21.
15   In Patrick's *Confession*, Victoricus is simply a man seen in a vision.
16   Jonah 1.17.
17   Exodus 15.24.
18   Exodus 16.13, Numbers 11.31.
19   Matthew 3.4.
20   1 Corinthians 10.28.
21   Ephesians 4.13.
22   The pope in Rome.
23   Bishop of Auxerre (southeast of Paris), he traveled to Britain in 429 and
     again several years later to combat the Pelagian heresy.
24   Acts 22.3.
25   *Voclut* in Patrick's *Confession*.
26   Pope from 422 to 432, he sent Palladius to Ireland as its first bishop in 431.
27   John 3.27.
28   Probably Amator, bishop of Auxerre before Germanus.
29   John 18.4.
30   Genesis 14.18, Psalm 110.4, Hebrews 5.6, 6.20, 7.1–22.
31   The poem speaks of a tonsured bishop with his pastoral staff or crosier
     standing at the front of a church celebrating the Eucharist while the con-
     gregation responds "Amen, Amen."
32   Slemish Mountain in County Antrim.
33   The region of Egypt where the Israelites settled (Genesis 45.10) and
     celebrated the first Passover (Exodus 12). The contest between Moses
     and Pharaoh (Exodus 5–12), aided by his magicians, is one source for the
     story that follows.
34   Psalm 74.13–14.
35   Daniel 3.
36   Daniel 6.6.

37 Matthew 2.3.
38 Psalm 20.7.
39 Psalm 68.1.
40 John 20.19.
41 Genesis 15.6, Romans 4.3.
42 John 18.4.
43 The contest is based on the battle between Elijah and the prophets of the god Baal (1 Kings 18.17–40).
44 Matthew 28.19–20.
45 The tyrant Coroticus of Patrick's letter.
46 Acts 7.55.
47 Probably the Isle of Man.
48 This seems to be a phrase in Patrick's native British language, meaning "by the God of judgment" (Jackson, *Language and History in Early Britain,* 633).
49 *Grazacham* in the text, apparently a corruption of Latin *gratias agamus* "Let us give thanks" (Jackson, *Language and History in Early Britain,* 145).
50 Saturday night.
51 Judges 6.36–40.
52 Exodus 3.2.
53 The same angel as Victoricus earlier in the story.
54 Matthew 19.28.
55 As with Moses (Deuteronomy 34.7).
56 A saying of uncertain origin.
57 2 Kings 20.8–11.
58 Joshua 10.12.
59 Genesis 27.27.
60 2 Kings 6.18.

THE LIFE OF SAINT BRIGID

1 As with the beginning of Muirchú's *Life of Saint Patrick*, compare the preface to the gospel of Luke (1.1–4).

2   1 Kings 17.8–16.

3   Romans 8.29.

4   Another early Latin life of Brigid, the *Vita I*, states that Brigid was the daughter of a Leinster nobleman Dubthach and his slave-woman Broicsech.

5   In early Ireland, butter was a labor-intensive luxury food not normally given to lower-class visitors (Kelly, *Early Irish Farming*, 325–327). This is the first of several episodes in which Brigid fulfills the biblical command to feed the poor (e.g., Deuteronomy 15.7, Matthew 5.42).

6   The first of several undiminished or restored food miracles in the *Life* based on biblical stories such as Moses and the manna in the wilderness (Exodus 16), the previously noted story of Elijah and the widow (1 Kings 17.8–16), and especially Jesus feeding the five/four thousand (Matthew 14.13–21, 15.29–39, Mark 6.30–44, 8.1–10, Luke 9.10–17, John 6.1–15).

7   The Latin *lardum* ("bacon, ham") of the text was, like butter, a mark of the Irish upper classes and a sign of prosperity (Kelly, *Early Irish Farming*, 336).

8   With Ireland's notoriously wet weather, this is an inversion of the miracles normally found in the Bible (e.g., 1 Kings 18.41–46) in which a lack of rain is alleviated by God.

9   In medieval Ireland, cows were normally milked twice a day, once in the morning and again in the evening (Kelly, *Early Irish Farming*, 40).

10   The power of a person over the sun is a frequent motif in folklore. It also occurs on a grander scale in the Hebrew Bible when the sun is made to stand still or move backward (Joshua 10.12–14, Isaiah 38.7–8).

11   Brigid's treatment of the clever thief echoes the gospel message of forgiving sinners seven times (Luke 17.4, Matthew 18.21–22). A *wether* is a castrated male sheep.

12   Leprosy is frequently mentioned in the Bible, including the New Testament miracles of Jesus (e.g., Luke 17.11–19).

13   John 2.1–11. Wine was an expensive import into Ireland, but beer was a common drink among even the lower classes (Kelly, *Early Irish Farming*, 319, 332–335).

14   A problematic passage given that abortion was consistently condemned by early Christian writers and was considered as grounds for divorce in Irish law (Kelly, *Early Irish Law*, 75), but the miracle is best seen as one of

healing and restoration to the Christian community rather than viewed in modern clinical terms. An interesting parallel is found in the Irish *Life of Saint Ciarán* in which the male saint makes the sign of the cross over the womb of a nun who has been raped and also causes the fetus inside her to vanish.

15 Mark 9.23, Matthew 17.20.

16 As with butter and bacon, salt was a valuable commodity in early Ireland. It is likely most Irish salt was made by burning and boiling seaweed, but it was also imported in cakes from abroad (Kelly, *Early Irish Farming*, 340–42). Salt in the New Testament is a metaphor for goodness (e.g., Matthew 5.13, Mark 9.49–50, Colossians 4.6).

17 Matthew 9.27–31, 20.29–34, Mark 8.22–26, 10.46–52, Luke 18.35–43, John 9.

18 John 8.12, 9.5.

19 Matthew 5.14.

20 John 14.12.

21 Matthew 13.31–32, 17.20, Mark 4.30–32, Luke 13.18–19.

22 Colossians 4.6.

23 Matthew 19.14, Mark 10.14, Luke 18.16.

24 Mark 9.14–29.

25 Dogs were important in early Ireland, particularly for their ability to guard a household or settlement (Kelly, *Early Irish Farming*, 114–21). They also serve this role in Irish literature, such as when the young hero Cú Chulainn takes his name from a ferocious hound and, in the *Scéla Muicce Meicc Dá Thó*, a hound guards all of Leinster.

26 Matthew 5.42.

27 Cattle were of crucial importance in medieval Irish society and an ongoing source of wealth and sustenance for the owner. A milk cow was a basic unit of currency on the island and would have been the standard annual rent paid by a prosperous farmer to his lord (Kelly, *Early Irish Law*, 10, 113; *Early Irish Farming*, 27–66).

28 Chariots are frequently mentioned in classical descriptions of battle among the Celtic peoples of continental Europe and Britain, as well as in early Irish stories. There is little archaeological evidence of chariots in Ireland, but such wooden constructions would not be likely to survive the centuries (Raftery, *Pagan Celtic Ireland*, 104–7).

29 The situation of a cow caring for a calf not its own was not as unusual as the *Life* makes it seem. Early Irish law deals with the situation in some detail (Kelly, *Early Irish Farming*, 545–551).

30 Luke 18.2.

31 Cattle raiding across tribal borders occurs frequently in the literature and history of medieval Ireland for replenishing stock and as an opportunity for warriors to prove their skill and bravery. Later monasteries were major centers of cattle raising and frequent targets of raids, so it is reasonable to suppose they were as well in the days of Cogitosus (Kelly, *Early Irish Farming*, 27–29, 167–168).

32 Genesis 7.21–23, Exodus 14.28.

33 The chariots described in early Irish literature seemed to have been simple two-wheeled vehicles pulled by two horses yoked to a pole in front (Raftery, *Pagan Celtic Ireland,* 105–106). A chariot miracle also occurs in Adomnan's *Life of Saint Columba* (2.43).

34 An *óenach* in Old Irish, normally called by a tribal king, during which there was often storytelling, feasting, and contests.

35 John 4.48, Romans 15.19.

36 Wild pigs were dangerous creatures and common in the woods of medieval Ireland. They differed little from their domesticated cousins, whose bones comprise nearly a third of the animal remains found at early Christian sites (Kelly, *Early Irish Farming*, 79–88, 281–282). Domestic adult pigs of the period, which unlike most modern varieties were small, long-legged, and hairy, were often allowed to feed in the forest until autumn when many would be slaughtered.

37 Job 5.23, Isaiah 11.6–9, 65.25, Ezekiel 34.25, Hosea 2.18.

38 Wolves are portrayed in the Bible in a negative sense whether as predators in a pastoral society or symbolic representatives of evil (e.g., Matthew 7.15, John 10.12, Acts 20.28–30). In medieval Ireland wolves were a serious threat to livestock. They are tamed by saints in a number of stories (Kelly, *Early Irish Farming*, 38–39, 186–187).

39 In folklore of many cultures and literatures, including the Bible (e.g., Luke 13.32), foxes are cunning and clever creatures. In early Ireland the fox, like the wolf above, was also a predator of farm animals and was viewed as a threat to livestock. Foxes were, however, sometimes

kept as pets, including one owned by Saint Mo Ling whom the holy man fed with his own hands (Kelly, *Early Irish Farming*, 124–25, 130–31, 188).

40 Colossians 1.16.

41 Matthew 13.1–9, 18–23.

42 Matthew 17.20, 21.21, Mark 11.23, Luke 17.6, 1 Corinthians 13.2.

43 In Irish law, a free person could be reduced to slavery if they could not pay a debt. To become a slave, whether male (*mug*) or female (*cumal*), was to lose all individual rights (Kelly, *Early Irish Law*, 95–97).

44 Numbers 35.6–32, Joshua 20.3.

45 The motif of a treasure found inside a fish is also widespread, most notably in the ancient Greek story of the ring of Polycrates (Herodotus 3.40–43). This miracle of Brigid also draws on the gospel story of the coin in the fish's mouth (Matthew 17.24–27).

46 Romans 12.13, Hebrews 13.2.

47 Weaving was the task of women in early Ireland and an essential contribution to the household (Kelly, *Early Irish Farming*, 449). The loss of one's loom was a prelude to destitution.

48 Another supreme gift of hospitality as well as celebratory gesture (Luke 15.23).

49 Silver was mined in Ireland and crafted into beautiful native vessels by skilled smiths. The metal was also used as currency (Kelly, *Early Irish Farming*, 435–36; *Early Irish Law*, 63, 114).

50 The main character in the biblical book of the same name, Job was noted for his righteousness (Job 1.1) and generosity in early Christian literature.

51 Brigid values the biblical injunction to clothe the poor (Job 31.19, Ezekiel 18.16, Matthew 25.36, Luke 3.11) more than the liturgical raiment.

52 A major holy day of the church liturgical year, such as Easter, Pentecost, or Christmas.

53 An evening worship service before the feast day of one of the apostles of Christ.

54 The celebration of the Eucharist.

55 Honey was a valuable food in medieval Ireland for its sweetening qualities, its use in making mead, and for its medicinal properties (Kelly, *Early Irish Farming*, 113).

56 Building roads across the treacherous bogs of Ireland was a major undertaking requiring great communal effort (Kelly, *Early Irish Farming*, 390–393; Raftery, *Pagan Celtic Ireland,* 98–104).

57 There were over a hundred tribes in early Ireland (Kelly, *Early Irish Laws,* 3–4). A powerful king could command the loyalty of a number of tribes and call the people of each to his service.

58 The difficult work of grinding grain into flour was traditionally performed by female slaves by hand on a quern. Once water mills were introduced in medieval Ireland, they became essential to the local economy (Kelly, *Early Irish Farming*, 245, 482–485).

59 This may be one of the Red Hills near Kildare, which contain gritty rock suitable for a millstone (Connolly and Picard, "Cogitosus's *Life of Brigit*," 6).

60 Castrated male cattle, when properly trained, were used for plowing and moving heavy loads in medieval Ireland (Kelly, *Early Irish Farming*, 48–49).

61 This passage provides one of the most detailed descriptions of an early Irish church, though scholars have long debated on the exact layout of the building. Although the sexes were separated by partitions, it is remarkable that at Kildare men and women worshipped together, unlike at some other churches (Harrington, *Women in a Celtic Church,* 75–80). In emphasizing the rich ornamentation of the church, Cogitosus is emphasizing the wealthy patronage of the church and its widespread support.

62 Although not a city in the modern sense, the community around Kildare and other monasteries would have been significant given the rural character of early Ireland.

63 The feast day of Brigid is also the day of the pre-Christian festival of Imbolc, which marked the birth of lambs and the lactating of ewes.

64 John 21.24–25.

THE VOYAGE OF SAINT BRENDAN

1 Revelation 21.23.
2 Psalm 145.17.

3 Jesus gives this new commandment to his disciples, that they should love one another (John 13.34).

4 In the *Rule of Saint Benedict* (chapter 3), an abbot is advised to seek the counsel of his monks before making an important decision. An *oratory* is a building other than a church set aside for prayer.

5 Mathew 19.29, Mark 10.29.

6 Jesus fasts for forty days in the wilderness (Matthew 4.2), though here Brendan divides the fast into smaller periods.

7 Also known as Éanna, his church was on Inishmore in the Aran Islands.

8 Such boats in the British Isles were known to Roman authors. For a description of a modern effort to re-create such a boat, see Tim Severin, *The Brendan Voyage*. Also very useful is James Hornell, *British Coracles and Irish Curraghs*.

9 The devil often appears in the form of an Ethiopian boy in hagiographical literature, as in the *Life of Saint Anthony* (section 6).

10 Luke 4.34.

11 The Thursday before Easter.

12 The day before Easter.

13 Exodus 12.5.

14 Fifty days after Easter.

15 The story of a whale mistaken for an island is found in many stories beyond Ireland, including a similar tale in the first voyage of Sinbad.

16 Islands of birds are a common motif in Irish voyage tales (Selmer, *Navigatio Sancti Brendani Abbatis* 86, n31) and reflect the reality of many small islands in the north Atlantic.

17 Lucifer, the devil, who rebelled against God and was cast out of heaven. These birds are angels who sided with Lucifer reluctantly.

18 Psalm 65.1.

19 Psalm 51.15.

20 Psalm 148.2.

21 Psalm 90.17.

22 Psalm 47.6.

23 Psalm 80.3, 7, 19.

24 Psalm 133.1.

25 Psalm 65.6.

26 Traditionally, Ailbe was a missionary who preached in the south of Ireland before St. Patrick.

27 A *paten* is a plate used to hold the bread of the Eucharist.

28 A *cruet* is a bottle used to hold wine and water for the Eucharist.

29 Psalm 38.22.

30 Baruch 2.12, Psalm 106.6.

31 Exodus 3.2.

32 Epiphany is traditionally January 6th in the western Christian church.

33 Revelation 7.10.

34 Psalm 118.27.

35 Matthew 8.26.

36 1 Samuel 17.

37 Psalm 84.7.

38 Psalm 67.1.

39 Psalm 69.1.

40 Psalm 116.10.

41 Psalm 130.1.

42 Psalm 133.1.

43 Psalm 147.12.

44 Psalm 65.1.

45 Psalm 103.1.

46 Psalm 133.1.

47 Psalms 120–34.

48 Psalm 148.1.

49 Psalm 149.1.

50 Psalm 150.1.

51 Psalm 51.1.

52 Psalm 63.1.

53 Psalm 90.1.

54 Psalm 47.2.

55 Psalm 54.1.

56 Psalm 116.1.

57 A mythological creature with the body of a lion and the head and wings of an eagle.

58 June 29.

59 Ezekiel 40–41, Revelation 21.10–11.
60 The disciple who betrayed Jesus (Matthew 26.14–25, 27.3–10, Mark 14.10–11, 43–46, Luke 22.47–48, John 18.2–3).
61 The king who tried to have Jesus killed as an infant (Matthew 2.1–22).
62 Pontius Pilate, Roman governor of Judaea, presided over the trial of Jesus and sentenced him to be crucified (Matthew 27, Mark 15.1–15, Luke 23.1–25, John 18.28–19.38).
63 Former Jewish high priest involved in the arrest of Jesus (John 18.13).
64 Jewish high priest who advised the council of priests that it was better for Jesus to die than for the whole nation be destroyed (John 18.14).
65 Psalm 133.1.
66 Psalm 65.5.
67 Psalm 84.4.

BIBLIOGRAPHY

Bieler, Ludwig. "The Hymn of St. Secundinus." *Proceedings of the Royal Irish Academy* 55.C.6 (1953): 117–27.

Bieler, Ludwig. *The Works of St. Patrick*. New York: Newman Press, 1953.

Bieler, Ludwig. *The Irish Penitentials*. Dublin: Dublin Institute for Advanced Studies, 1975.

Bieler, Ludwig. *Libri Epistolarum Sancti Episcopi*. Dublin: Royal Irish Academy, 1993.

Bieler, Ludwig. *The Patrician Texts in the Book of Armagh*. Dublin: Dublin Institute for Advanced Studies, 2000.

Bitel, Lisa. *Isle of the Saints: Monastic Settlement and Christian Community in Early Ireland*. Ithaca, NY: Cornell University Press, 1990.

Bitel, Lisa. *Landscape with Two Saints: How Genovefa of Paris and Brigit of Kildare Built Christianity in Barbarian Europe*. Oxford: Oxford University Press, 2009.

Carey, John, Herbert, Máire, and Ó Riain, Pádraig, eds. *Saints and Scholars*. Dublin: Four Courts Press, 2001

Cartwright, Jane, ed. *Celtic Hagiography and Saints' Cults*. Cardiff: University of Wales Press, 2003.

Conneely, Daniel. *St. Patrick's Letters: A Study of Their Theological Dimension*. Maynooth, Ireland: An Sagart, 1993.

Connolly, Sean, and Picard, J.-M. "Cogitosus's *Life of St. Brigit*." *The Journal of the Royal Society of Antiquaries of Ireland* 117 (1987): 5–27.

Davies, Oliver, and O'Loughlin, Thomas. *Celtic Spirituality*. New York: Paulist Press, 1999.

De Paor, Liam. *Saint Patrick's World*. Notre Dame, IN: University of Notre Dame Press, 1993.

Dumville, David. *Saint Patrick: A.D. 493–1993*. Rochester, NY: The Boydell Press, 1993.

Faris, M. J., ed. *The Bishops' Synod*. Liverpool: Francis Cairns, 1976.

Freeman, Philip. *Ireland and the Classical World*. Austin: University of Texas Press, 2001.

Freeman, Philip. *War, Women, and Druids: Eyewitness Reports and Early Accounts of the Ancient Celts*. Austin: University of Texas Press, 2002.

Freeman, Philip. *St. Patrick of Ireland: A Biography*. New York: Simon & Schuster, 2004.

Hanson, Richard P. C. *Saint Patrick: His Origins and Career*. Oxford: Oxford University Press, 1968.

Hanson, Richard P. C., and Blanc, Cécile. *Confession et la lettre à Coroticus*. Paris: Les Éditions du Cerf, 1978.

Harmless, William. *Desert Christians: An Introduction to the Literature of Early Monasticism*. Oxford: Oxford University Press, 2004.

Harrington, Christina. *Women in a Celtic Church: Ireland 450–1150*. Oxford: Oxford University Press, 2002.

Herbert, Máire. *Iona, Kells, and Derry*. Dublin: Four Courts Press, 1996.

Hood, A. B. E. *St. Patrick: His Writings and Muirchu's Life*. London: Phillimore, 1978.

Hornell, James. *British Coracles and Irish Curraghs*. London: Society for Nautical Research, 1938.

Hughes, Kathleen. *Early Christian Ireland: Introduction to the Sources*. Cambridge: Cambridge University Press, 1972.

Hughes, Kathleen, and Hamlin, Ann. *The Modern Traveller to the Early Irish Church*. Dublin: Four Courts Press, 1997.

Jackson, Kenneth. *Language and History in Early Britain*. Edinburgh: Edinburgh University Press, 1953.

Kelly, Fergus. *A Guide to Early Irish Law*. Dublin: Dublin Institute for Advanced Studies, 1988.

Kelly, Fergus. *Early Irish Farming*. Dublin: Dublin Institute for Advanced Studies, 2000.

Kenney, James. *The Sources for the Early History of Ireland: Ecclesiastical*. New York: Columbia University Press, 1929.

Koch, John, and Carey, John, eds. *The Celtic Heroic Age*. Aberystwyth, Wales: Celtic Studies Publications, 2003.

Mac Coitir, Niall. *Ireland's Animals: Myths, Legends, and Folklore*. Cork: The Collins Press, 2010.

McCone, Kim. *Pagan Past and Christian Present in Early Irish Literature*. Maynooth, Ireland: An Sagart, 1991.

Meyer, Kuno. *The Voyage of Bran*. London: David Nutt, 1895.

Nagy, Joseph. *Conversing with Angels and Ancients*. Ithaca, NY: Cornell University Press, 1997.

Ó Cróinín, Dáibhí. *Early Medieval Ireland: 400–1200*. London: Longman, 1995.

Ó hAodha, Donncha, ed. *Bethu Brigte*. Dublin: Dublin Institute for Advanced Studies, 1978.

O'Loughlin, Thomas. *St. Patrick: The Man and His Works*. London: Triangle, 1999.

O'Loughlin, Thomas. *Celtic Theology*. London: Continuum, 2000.

O'Loughlin, Thomas. *Discovering Saint Patrick*. New York: Paulist Press, 2005.

O'Meara, John J. *The Voyage of Saint Brendan*. Buckinghamshire, England: Colin Smythe Ltd., 1991.

Ó Riain, Pádraig. *A Dictionary of Irish Saints*. Dublin: Four Courts Press, 2011.

Raftery, Barry. *Pagan Celtic Ireland*. London: Thames and Hudson, 1994.

Rivet, A. L. F., and Smith, Colin. *The Place-Names of Roman Britain*. London: Batsford Ltd., 1979.

Selmer, Carl. *Navagatio Sancti Brendani Abbatis*. Dublin: Four Courts Press, 1989.

Severin, Tim. *The Brendan Voyage*. New York: Modern Library, 2000.

Sharpe, Richard. *Medieval Irish Saints' Lives*. Oxford: Clarendon Press, 1991.

Snyder, Christopher. *Exploring the World of King Arthur*. London: Thames and Hudson, 2011.

Stokes, Whitley, and Strachan, John, eds. *Thesaurus Paleohibernicus*. Dublin: Dublin Institute for Advanced Studies, 1975.

Thom, Catherine. *Early Irish Monasticism*. London: T&T Clark, 2006.

Thompson, E. A. *Who Was Saint Patrick?* Rochester, NY: Boydell Press, 1985.

Webb, J. F., trans., and Farmer, D. H., ed. *The Age of Bede*. New York: Penguin Books, 1998.

White, Newport J. D. *Libri Sancti Patricii*. Dublin: University of Dublin Press, 1905.

Wooding, Jonathan M. *The Otherworld Voyage in Early Irish Literature*. Dublin: Four Courts Press, 2000.

INDEX